Disrupting Partisan Politics

Finding Humanity in a World of Hyper Partisanship

The Story of the 2023 Yemi for Mayor Campaign

Military Might Publishing - militarymightpublishing.com

Publisher's Cataloging-in-Publication Data

Names: Cicak, Niki (Tonya Nikole), 1979- .

Title: Disrupting partisan politics : finding humanity in a world of hyper partisanship / Niki Cicak.

Description: Colorado Springs, CO : Military Might Publishing, 2024. | Includes 1 b&w diagram. | Summary: The story of Nigerian-American Yemi Mobolade's 2023 campaign for mayor of Colorado Springs, CO. His Republican campaign manager Niki Cicak and his Democratic political strategist Anthony Carlson were able to bring the city together, disrupting partisan politics and winning the election.

Identifiers: ISBN 9781961019195 (pbk.)

Subjects: LCSH: Mobolade, Yemi, 1979- . | Local elections – Colorado – Colorado Springs. | Two-party systems – United States. | Colorado Springs (Colo.) – Politics and government. | BISAC: POLITICAL SCIENCE / American Government / Local. | POLITICAL SCIENCE / Political Process / Campaigns & Elections. | POLITICAL SCIENCE / Political Ideologies / Democracy.

Classification: LCC JS785.C53 2024 | DDC 320.8 C--dc23

Disrupting Partisan Politics

Finding Humanity in a World of Hyper Partisanship

Niki Cicak

Military Might Publishing

Dedication

This book is dedicated to all those brave citizens who stand up for change. Who see a path forward to a country run for the people by the people. To those who get involved, let your voice be heard and VOTE! Be the agent of change in your communities.

To all those on the campaign team who sacrificed sleep, days off, time with their families and so much more. Thank you! Your dedication to this campaign did not go unnoticed. Your passion, drive and courage made the difference.

To my family, for your patience and understanding. For your never-ending support and encouragement. Thank you for always supporting my ambitions and dreams.

And to Yemi. You are first my friend, and I am so proud of you. You have become the mayor we all knew you could be. Thank you for what you have and are doing for our city. Thank you for your leadership, passion and for your servant's heart. From the bottom of my heart, thank you for this opportunity to be a part of this incredible journey and for the chance to lead the hardest working team in politics.

Words from the Team

"Niki and Anthony are the dynamic duo of campaigning. They took a candidate who was single digits in name recognition and brought him into a historic Mayoral win. Anthony's savvy strategy and Niki's team administration were the one-two punch we needed to galvanize a team of political newbies. I was honored to partner with them."

Thomas Thompson, CEO Thompson Leadership, Campaign Board Co-Chair

"Just when I thought politics was hopeless, along came Yemi Mobolade, who is a once-in-a-lifetime inspirational leader, humble human being, and tireless candidate. It was clear to me that he should be our mayor, but most thought it would be impossible to get him elected. Then along came Anthony and Niki. Anthony's strategic brilliance combined with Niki's get-it-done-no-nonsense work ethic was the perfect compliment to Yemi's people-first approach to politics. They pulled off a miracle and turned my hopelessness into hopefulness. They turned me into a believer that American politics can work again.

They convinced me that if we care enough to participate and do the hard work, then we can derail the divisive political freight train we are riding today.

I am an entrepreneur who has enjoyed success in the private sector. But by far, participating in Yemi's campaign for Mayor was one of the most satisfying projects I've ever taken on, and I am immensely proud of the work we did to help change the course of politics in America."

Mike Juran, CEO of Altia, Campaign Board Co-Chair

"Being a part of this campaign was a highlight of my career. Watching this city come together as one unified community behind Yemi was nothing short of awe-inspiring. I truly believe that the hiring of Niki and Anthony was a game changer and set us on a path to a win!"

Vance Brown, Co-Founder & CEO of Exponential Impact, Lawyer & Entrepreneur

"Niki's book provides an authoritative, behind-the-scenes look at one of the nation's most exciting mayoral campaigns. With an unlikely team of heroes, Yemi Mobolade was able to pull off an upset that shifted the power dynamics in Colorado Springs for good. Niki and Anthony's leadership, grit, and experience provided the perfect blend to guide the campaign of an unaffiliated candidate through potential dangers, traps, and snares that resulted in a campaign and a mayor free from partisan chaos. Niki provides a thoughtful and inspiring look at a story that restores hope to American politics and challenges us all to think bigger than red or blue."

Joe Hollmann, Chair of Communications Team, Campaign Volunteer

"I had never before experienced an environment that encompassed the highest levels of data, relevant information, relationships, respect and appreciation all in the same room. Niki and Anthony pulled together and led a team that was a joy to be a part of, and it worked!"

Susan Pattee, Entrepreneur, Philanthropist and Campaign Board Member

"Working on the campaign team alongside Niki and Anthony was an invaluable experience, as their leadership and dedication inspired everyone to work towards a common goal. Witnessing the unity among our diverse team members not only fostered a sense of belonging but also displayed the strength that comes from embracing different perspectives and backgrounds. Together, we were able to achieve more than we ever could have individually, leaving a lasting impact on both the campaign and our shared vision for the future."

Niki Fields, Yemi for Mayor Campaign Volunteer

"What I love about this work is helping to empower people to be involved in something they can be proud of. I make it my personal goal to help eliminate any obstacle I can for volunteers. And Niki is the definition of Boss. She was the glue that held all the separate parts of the campaign together. And she did it with an infectious joy and excitement that inspired us. She showed respect for different ideas and suggestions but kept us all focused on the goals of the campaign. The way she gives constructive feedback or redirects good intentions towards productivity is an art form. The way she made things happen was awe-inspiring."

Abbi Groft-Kelly, Lead Field Coordinator Yemi for Mayor Campaign

Contents

Preface

The minute we won the 2023 Colorado Springs Mayoral Race, I told Anthony, our campaign strategist, that this story must be told. I told him we must tell other communities that what we did here is possible, and it is possible in cities across this nation. No matter the backgrounds or what 'has always been,' there is always a path forward for positive change and, most importantly, for hope.

While I was not a person who would have ever said I had political aspirations before this campaign, that all changed the day Yemi, and I discussed his joining the race for the 42nd Mayor of Colorado Springs. Although I always knew I would work in advocacy, I was not always certain what that would look like. One of my favorite aspects of being Yemi's Campaign Manager was the unity we were able to restore in this city and in politics overall. Even my own mother would tell you I was always the kid that wanted all my friends to be friends. I am an open book, and I always loved being on a team, working for a common goal.

Our country is hurting, and really our world. We have used divisiveness for personal gain and as a distraction from political issues for far too long. I believe in the depth of my soul that we can be better, do better. That we can feel completely different about an issue and yet be respectful and kind in our disagreement. Trust me, this does not mean becoming complacent or failing to stand for something. As the saying goes, 'If you do not stand for something, you will fall for anything.' Whoever first said that was a brilliant human being! We choose to forget that there is more that unites us as a society than divides us. We often choose to believe the 'noise' that has been strategically placed to keep us fighting among ourselves. All the while overlooking certain behaviors and actions that are taking place right before our very eyes. Be assured, this is by design.

I have always worked very hard to unite anyone and everyone around me. It pains me to see what has happened to the America I love so deeply. But we are not a lost cause, quite the opposite. If this campaign proved anything, it is that people want better: better discussions, better collaboration, and a better path toward unity. They are speaking out that they are ready to find common ground and work to better our societies and our world. We must stop this mentality that "my vote doesn't matter" or that "I'm just so sick of them all, and all that fighting that I stay out of it." Good people MUST get involved to make change for the good. My hope for this book is to inspire communities across the nation—and perhaps even around the globe—to replicate what we did here, to demand more from their governments, and to unite for the good of their communities.

Forward

The 2023 Victory Speech of Yemi Mobolade as the 42nd Mayor of Colorado Springs

"Thank you! Wow, this is my family. Wow, I amspeechless. My heart is still pounding. I am shocked and I have the best view in the house. I really do. This is incredible. Thank you, (Yemi says to Abbey and his children. Gives Abbey a kiss, as she walks off the stage with their kids). Thank you, wow, I love you guys! Oh man, I see so many incredible people in the house. I wish I could just call you all by names, because that is really what I want to do.

This is our win! We are Colorado Springs! Friends, it is a new day in our beloved City. Do you believe that because I do? It is a new day and tonight, just like we did six weeks ago in the same room, we stand on a mountain of a new era in our city's history. Colorado Springs will become an inclusive culturally rich, economically prosperous, safe, and vibrant city on a hill that shines brightly. You, the voters, have spoken, and you have chosen your next mayor. Friends, our city is hungry as represented by this room tonight. We are ready for leadership that represents all of our city, and I am ready to serve as your 42nd Mayor of Colorado Springs, of this beautiful, resilient and passionate city, of which I am very fond of. Who else is fond of this city? That is what I am talking about. You see, to anyone who doubts that politics can be disrupted, reformed, and transformed into a hopeful experience, tonight is for you. To the citizen who has lost hope in this great experiment and a dream of our founders, what we call the United States of America, tonight is for you. To one in this room who is in utter disbelief that Republicans and Democrats and Independents can work together, can find common ground, maybe even like each other, tonight is for you. Because we are Colorado Springs, it is who we are and how we get stuff done.

Friends, we have accomplished everything we said we were going to do. One, we said we are going to run a campaign full of hope and inspiration and optimism and we did that. Two, we said we will put your quality of life ahead of party politics and we did that. And three, we said we are going to unite ourselves around the common purpose of city and citizen greatness and we did that. We did that! And we did it with courage, and empathy, and humility, and we did it together, because we are Colorado Springs.

Friends, it has been a long, hard journey. No campaign has worked harder, and I am confident about that. I see you all in the room. A lot of people working hard alongside me. So, I need to say some thank you's to the people who walked and climbed and sometimes clawed with me throughout this journey.

First, to my amazing wife Abbey. I told you she was a badass. Friends, raising three kids under 10 years old, while working, and while your husband is gone most of the time, relentlessly running a campaign. There is nothing less than badass about that. And she will be a badass first lady just for the record.

To my kids, all the bedtimes that I missed because of a busy dad. I know you are little, and I hope you see, this is for you because one day this city will be yours and I promise that I will do my best to make this city into a great city, not just for my kids but for your kids and your grandkids as well.

To my campaign team, Niki (Campaign Manager), where are you? We call her the hammer. My chief political strategist, Anthony, wherever you are, thank you. Joe, wherever you are, my communications director, Joe, well done. You all went far and above what was needed for this campaign, and I am not sure that you got sleep either. I am forever grateful.

And to the rest of my campaign team and my campaign board – Abby, Shelby, Alexis, Moni, Jen C, Jenn S, Tariro, Yemi Sanchez, Adam, Forrest, Jacob, Katie, Robin, Liam, Skyler, Isaac, Daniel, Cameron, Scott, Annie, Isaac, Mike, Anna, Dan, Mallory, Jamie, Maureen, Deb, Susan, Donna, Tatiana, Thomas, Larry, Josh, Pastor Greg, Vance, Leaf, Mike, Thomas and Margaret Saban. I see you all and thank you, thank you, thank you, thank you, thank you.

I am also motivated by the heartfelt endorsement by many of our city's leaders and public servants and a couple of them are here tonight. Bill Elder, wherever you are, I am humbled to have your endorsement. This win is in part to you. Sally Clark, you too, I am humbled to have your endorsement. It takes a lot of courage for these two leaders. They see the Colorado Springs that I see, too. And I am grateful to you guys for your support. Friends, it takes a village. I have the most talented, dedicated and hard-working esteemed village that the city has ever seen. The gift of wisdom and dedication and leadership is truly second to none.

To the hundreds of volunteers in this room, who have helped me knock on, just about forty thousand doors, you have made phone calls, you have sent text messages, you have written postcards and over a thousand of you have donated funds to this campaign. Friends in this room who have hosted over a hundred meet and greets, I see you all. Supporters in this room and across the city who are spreading hope and optimism and helping to set the record straight on Facebook and Next Door. Thank you, thank you! I see you all. You know, I had a resident once tell me, your fans are stealth. You guys just move in and out of the city, setting the record straight. Friends, my campaign success is because of you, make no mistake about it. I am because we are, I am because we are, I am because we are Colorado Springs!

Friends, tonight we celebrate but on June 6th, swearing-in day and the weeks leading up to it, the real work begins. And I am ready to deliver on my campaign promises. You told me you want safer neighborhoods and a fully staffed and well-trained police department. Innovative solutions to prevent and end homelessness. Let us get to work. You told me you want your city government to prioritize our growing infrastructure needs, and to strengthen our water infrastructure, and build more affordable and attainable housing. Let us get to work. You told me you wanted higher paying jobs and to build a more business friendly city, and to cut the red tape that locks out entrepreneurs and local visionaries. It is time. Let us get to work people. The voters have spoken today, and I am ready to work with you. I promised a more accessible government. I promised a more transparent government. I promised pragmatic and innovative solutions to meet the growing challenges that are in front of us, and that is exactly what I am going to do. Let us get to work.

To those of you who did not vote for me tonight or who did not even vote, I promise to be a mayor for all people. I am going to keep that promise. So, I look forward to hearing your voices, your needs, your pain points, and your ideas, too, because they matter. Friends, I received a gracious and generous call from Wayne Williams. He conceded, and he thanked me. Can we give it up for Wayne as well? He fought a hard, long journey like I did. He fought even harder for our community and for our state, in the years of service that he has served our city. Friends, as I close, I have to bring attention to Old Glory. This flag symbolizes, and that name symbolizes, our ancient values of freedom, democracy, the competition of ideas, diversity, compromise, and unity. You see, the color red represents courage. The color blue symbolizes justice. And the color white symbolizes purity. So, you can expect me to lead with red, courage, and expect me to fight for blue, justice, and because our moment in history calls for renewed optimism and hope, I will lead with white and purify our city from the Washington DC agendas. There is a new way politics can be done, and that starts today. That starts today!

In this journey, I have received so many encouraging words from many of you in this room. From the retired Air Force officer Chuck Smith, who said to me, I was in the military, I know leadership. Yemi, you have leadership, keep going. To the couple I met at a meet and greet, at FH Beerworks, who said we have lived in this community for 45 years, you are the best since Mayor Bob Isaac. True story. What a compliment. To the many affirmations and pause around the positive and clean campaign that we have run right, we showed it can be done. Many of you have sent me messages, but I want to read one from a gentleman by the name of Matt Lin. He sent this to me just yesterday. 'Hey Yemi, I do not know if you remember me. My name is Matt Lin. I met you at the Jives in Old Colorado City, during one of your first meet and greets. You wholly inspired this city and the people to step into a new vision and heart, for what this city could be and that is incredible. No matter how this race ends, trust me, I have placed my bets on you. Just remember that you went from being the absolute underdog to uplifting the idea of what this city and the people could be. And that is worth so much more than politics.' And Matt ends his text to me by saying, 'I am continually praying for you and your family and this campaign, that this city could be the light on top of the hill. If we are supposed to be salt and light, we are going to need a salty leader.' I do not know if that is a compliment. Like salty leader, I had to look, I had to reread that one. I am like a salted leader and then he said,' My friend, you are the saltiest lead I have ever seen. Thank you so much for what you have done. I truly appreciate it.' Matt, thank you. To everyone in this room, thank you for your words of encouragement and affirmation. It means the world to me. I am because we are!

Finally, I would be remiss if I did not honor my family, who came out all the way from Houston, Texas. Happy Mother's Day, Mummy. My older brother Chris is here, and my youngest sister Bunmi is somewhere here. And I want to honor my dad, who actually flew internationally to get here in time for this. Okay, so check this out. I am going to brag a little bit. He arrived on Wednesday and took his citizenship test on Thursday and passed. He is the only one left in the family. It took you a while, Dad, so welcome to the club.

Friends, greater things are yet to come. Greater things are still to be done in this city. Let us carry this campaign energy and win for our city. Because it will take all of us in this room and all of us at home to make Colorado Springs into a world-class American city, because we are Colorado Springs.

Thank you for your support. May God bless your families. May God bless the great City of Colorado Springs, and may God bless the United States of America. Thank you so much! Onward and upward! Thank you!"

Yemi Mobolade, *42nd Mayor of Colorado Springs*

Introduction

Twelve contenders. Two advanced to the runoff.
$948,285 raised.

1,265 unique donors vs. our runoff opponent's 331.
$394.63 average donation vs. their $2,783.82.

110 meet-and-greets.
40,000 doors knocked.

Hundreds upon hundreds of yard signs. Thousands
of buttons shared.

Eight teams.
100+ dedicated volunteers.

One extraordinary candidate.

General Election Results:
Mobolade - 29.81% | Runoff opponent - 19.22%

Runoff Election Results:
Mobolade - 57.5% | Runoff opponent - 42.5%

One United City.

We were a young, new to politics, green team of enthusiastic people fighting for a common goal. We believed, no...we knew, that this city was ready to make a statement. To become a beacon to the rest of the country, a beacon to what is possible when people come together. Voters of all ages, political affiliations, and backgrounds united behind one candidate. But what they united behind was a message. A message that we can disagree, but still be friends. That we can express our passions and our viewpoints in a respectful manner. That we can listen to each other and work to understand the perspectives that brought us here. That we do not have to hang our hats on the 5% of issues that we differ on. There are 95% of things on which we have common ground, and we can focus on elevating those. That we do not have to be subjected to mudslinging and negative campaigning.

There will always be issues we as individuals will differ on. There will always be people who are pro-life and pro-choice. There will always be people who defend the Second Amendment and those who advocate for stricter gun control laws, among other issues. But if I have learned anything in my forty-plus years, it is that fighting, bickering, and name-calling never change opposing opinions. There is such a thing as healthy conflict. Great ideas are born from healthy conflict. Healthy conflict fosters an environment for conversation, idea sharing, and resolution discovery. Polarization has solved nothing. In my observation, the rise of severe polarization over the past 15 years has been driven by specific agendas. I cannot remember another time in my life where animosity was so prevalent. We must stop this and get back to the point of healthy dialogue.

We have lost the art of healthy debate and trying to understand the *why* that brought this person to feeling the way they do today. We do not take the time to learn each other's story, because if we did.... God forbid...we might find similarities in our stories. My belief is that the more we focus on becoming better versions of ourselves and on actions for which we will be accountable, the less time we have available to breakdown someone else. I do not know about you, but I have plenty of work to do for myself and my own personal growth. If we as American citizens would get up and become more involved in our communities, instead of being couch quarterbacks, convinced we could do better, we might actually learn a few things. Hey, if you think you can do it better, get up and show me! I am eager to learn from what you know. Working together is how we get things done!

"To one in this room who is in utter disbelief that republicans, democrats and independents can work together, can find common ground - maybe even like each other! Tonight is for you!" These were the words Yemi excitedly uttered during his election night speech. This campaign proved it can be done—that partisan politics from Washington, D.C., has no place in Colorado Springs. That we can bridge the divide and work together to solve problems. What we want everyone to see is that you, too, can do this in any

community across the country. That you can be the next example of disagreeing better and work to end the divisiveness in hometowns across the nation. That a new trend can emerge, reflecting what the American people are truly asking for.

While writing this book, I learned of an initiative being spearheaded by Gov. Spencer Cox of Utah, Gov. Jared Polis of Colorado, and the National Governors Association (NGA) called *Disagree Better.* If you have not heard about this, please look it up. The work that they are doing speaks directly to the heart of what we did in Colorado Springs. In fact, while reading about the initiative, I had the thought, how are they reading my mind right now! This is exactly what we fought for...and succeeded in doing in Colorado Springs. *"We know that conflict resolution takes work and involves difficult conversations. It's much easier to sow division than to persuade or find solutions. But we also know that no one ever changed someone's mind by attacking them. Through healthy conflict, we're confident that we can find common ground and improve our families, our communities and our nation. Together, we can disagree better."* ~ Utah Governor Spencer Cox, NGA Chair (Taken from the Disagree Better Website, https://www.nga.org/disagree-better/). Preach Governor! You are singing my song! I look forward to the day where I get the opportunity to meet Gov. Cox and help advance the mission of the NGA's work. We share his message in the work we have done and continue to do in the city.

Change is not easy, we can attest, but at this point it is necessary. If we continue down this path, we will reach a stalemate where collaboration and resolution become impossible. We must do better. The future success of our nation depends on it.

Chapter One

Courage Empathy Humility
The Core Values

The etymology of words fascinates Yemi Mobolade. He carefully studies the meaning and origins of every word he chooses, considering how he can apply them in his life. There is meaning behind every choice, decision, or action he makes. He educates himself on every topic before him, actively engages in learning, and surrounds himself with experts on the relevant issues. He takes nothing for granted or makes decisions he knows affect people's lives lightly. This held true for every aspect of the campaign and even the philosophy that drove us. Courage, Empathy and Humility. These are his core values and the core values we adopted for the campaign. Everything we did, every decision we made, every conversation we had, focused on these three values.

Courage - *"Courage over comfort"*

The Oxford Dictionary defines courage as *"the ability to do something dangerous, or to face pain or opposition, without showing fear."* But when you delve deeper into its meaning, it encompasses much more. The root of the word is 'cor,' the Latin word for 'heart,' making its fundamental meaning 'a brave heart.' This resonated so much with me. Stepping into the political arena is not for the faint of heart. You will be attacked, people will make up things about you, even blatant lies at times. Because they want the same thing you do. You need thick skin and the courage to stay focused on the goal. Drown out the noise and stay the course. But more importantly, you must be courageous in your pursuit of good. You must be courageous in your actions and the work it takes to create a government that works for the whole of the people we serve. We live in a world where we are constantly encouraged to prioritize our own comfort. But the most courageous acts that we strive for take us out of that state and slam us right into the "uncomfortable" and what a great place to be. When you become "comfortable" in the "uncomfortable," the most amazing things happen.

The greatest personal growth takes place. You discover your true potential when you choose courage and fight for what you believe is right and good. When you are fighting to give a voice to the voiceless and truly listening to the needs of your community, you find a strength inside of yourself you may never have known was there. When you have a courageous heart, you see setbacks as only a speed bump on your path to justice. You see naysayers as the people you cannot wait to bring to your table of victory. But the best is when you see an opportunity to inspire, truly listen with intention and then muster the strength to keep fighting even when you think you have nothing left to give. This is the place where you find true personal growth. You find that resiliency you never thought you had. But this is the place where societal progress and the betterment of the community flourish. This is where true advocacy and community growth flourish.

At no point during this journey did I ever see a place where Yemi lost courage. In fact, I saw quite the opposite. His unending drive to stay the course, stay focused on the mission of unity and bring up everyone around him never wavered. Even in his most tiring moments on the campaign trail, he would say, "Schedule another meet and greet that day. Let us knock on ten more doors. Who needs me today to hear them and I'll listen." He never stopped. His courage inspired every single person on our team to do the same. There were days I did not think I could put one more foot in front of the other, and he would stand right by me, and we would pick each other up and push through. His drive and motivation spread to every single person on our team. We faced adversity and had to fight twice as hard at every step. But when you see his courage and his leadership, you know you could do it too.

My favorite part was watching that courage spread from our team to the entire city. We watched people follow us and step out of their comfort zones. We saw people of every background, every race, color, creed, political preference, every side of every issue you could imagine, rise together, and stand hand in hand to make sure we had a city that was not for the few, but for the many. They worked tirelessly next to each other, knocking on doors, writing cards, hosting meet and greets and standing next to each other at debates, as one courageous heart. Our city is a melting pot, and our campaign reflected that. Citizens showed that while we may disagree on topics, we can still be respectful, listen to each other, and engage in meaningful dialogue. It takes more courage than you can ever imagine to be respectful when in a conversation with a person who has opposite views, and we proved it can be done. People are hungry for conversations. They are hungry to feel like, even though we may not agree, we can stand together and fight for a city, a state or a country who hears us all. More importantly, they want leaders who will listen intently, consider both sides, and trust that we can find a 'third way'—a middle-ground solution. The third way does not have to be seen as compromising your morals or values. It is finding common ground and asking how we can be better together. One of my proudest moments was at the campaign kick-off event in early January 2023. A community leader walked up to us and said, "How in the world did you get these people in a room together? I don't know that I've ever seen some of these folks in the same room."

Courage

It takes courage to bring opposing people together in a room. It takes courage to lead through adversity. It takes courage to unify when we fight so hard to divide. It takes courage to bring your opponents to the same leadership table and ask, 'How can we improve together?' One of Yemi's greatest heroes is Abraham Lincoln. In any conversation about his leadership style or role models, Abraham Lincoln is always the first name he mentions. One of his favorite books is *"Team of Rivals"* by Doris Kearns Goodwin. If you have not read it, I highly recommend you do. Doris talks about the political genius of Lincoln's leadership style and how Lincoln built his cabinet with his opponents. He had respect for their differences and knew that if he brought them all together that they could lead the entire country and not just certain constituencies. Lincoln is still revered as one of America's greatest presidents and a leader who fought to reunify a country that was bleeding from division. He brought us through one of the greatest wars our country has ever seen, only to immediately get to work healing a divided nation. That takes courage. I like to think that Lincoln also led with empathy. He felt the broken hearts of this nation and knew that his immediate responsibility was to bring the nation back together. He knew the country needed to heal, and it was his job to lead the country out of that chapter and into a place of unity.

Empathy - *"Empathy over apathy"*

"I see you." I cannot count how many times I heard Yemi utter these words to not only me, but our entire team, citizens on the campaign trail and now to the entire city. I did not know, even within my heart, how powerful the words 'I see you' can be. The effect of having someone look you in the eye and tell you are seen, you are heard and 'I've got you' can be life altering. The etymology of the word "Empathy" derives from the Greek prefix *"En"* meaning "in" or within" and the noun *"pathos"* meaning "feeling" or "suffering." Therefore, the meaning of the word is to *"enter into someone else's suffering."* He talks about the value of empathy as the cornerstone to humanizing our work. When we talked about his platform during the campaign, one of my favorite things we talked about was "humanizing the badge" when talking about police and public safety. In a time where not everyone believed in backing the blue, we reminded people that behind that badge is a human being, with families they want to get home to as well. And in the same breath, we discussed his plans of increasing training and supporting our police force with the training necessary to protect our city. We had philosophies centered on the "both/and" mentality that two things can be true and we must work to find the solution that solves both problems. We talked about humanizing politics. That when we discuss an issue, we need to be reminded that we are discussing something that affects real people and the lives they are leading. We cannot forget that we are leading people, not fighting for our own agendas.

Now, people might make a variety of assumptions. On a mayoral level, there are a lot of hot-button issues that the mayor's office has no purview over. And that is ok. The responsibilities of that office consist of infrastructure, public parks and, of course, public safety. But that does not mean we cannot empathize with the constituents affected by these issues. In Colorado Springs, we have citizens who are concerned with the overwhelming growth of the city in a noticeably brief time span. While growth is good, living things must grow, cities need to have responsible growth, all the while, taking into consideration the effects on natural resources, public safety and having a strong plan for the effects on infrastructure. We have citizens concerned with where certain projects must be built. While we cannot always change the fact that a project needs to take place, we can look to help minimize disruption and the impact on the surrounding communities. This is where Yemi shines. His ability to bring to light the possibility of the fact that there can be a "both/and" approach to solving a constituent's issue is unseen elsewhere. He has an innate ability to hear all sides of an issue, empathize with everyone involved and somehow find the ability to balance that with the "third way" solution.

I think our ability to empathize with citizens of Colorado Springs was one of the most inspirational and powerful experiences of the campaign. We heard story after story of citizens who were fed up and frustrated because they felt they had not been listened to in years. They felt like the city was a city of the few. That the city was run by a small group of people who only focused on their own interests. They would tell us they understood you cannot please all the people all the time, but at least listen to our concerns and let us know they are even being considered. Residents would tell us all the time how much they just wanted the chance to be heard and to feel like someone cared about the issue, even if they could not get the resolution they desired. It is not always about achieving the desired outcome but about hearing concerns, taking them into consideration, and exploring all possible solutions. While Anthony Carlson (our campaign strategist) and I were meeting with one of our campaign advisors during the preparations for this book, she told us she remembers driving past the city admin building during our campaign and she remembered feeling sad at what had become. She said, "Imagine how much better this city will be with Yemi at the helm." She said, "I don't think that they did it intentionally. Maybe they didn't even realize, but they were disenfranchising people." She and our entire team felt that we needed a greater diversity of voices at the table. And the citizens agreed. Where Yemi excels is in his ability to bring a variety of leaders in different industries with diverse backgrounds together to solve a widespread problem. He differs from various leaders in that he does not feel he knows all the answers, but rallies teams of leaders to the table to work together to solve the issue. What he practices is genuine humility.

Humility - *"We before me."*

"I am, because WE are." Yemi closed every event, meeting or gathering with this phrase. And he meant it. He knows the importance of surrendering pride when in positions of leadership. Bet you know where I am heading next? That is right! The meaning of the word. The root of the word is from the Latin word *"humus"* meaning "the ground" or "the earth." Thus, translated as "being grounded." A state of being grounded or down-to-earth keeps a person balanced, level headed, and practical. When you are grounded, you create an environment conducive to foster collaboration. When you are humble, you listen, you value being a lifelong learner, you foster and recognize the contributions of others, and you maintain an internal sense of control and power. There were a million examples of how he practiced humility, but the overarching theme I resonated with the most is that he stayed in the trenches with the team the entire time. He never asked us to do anything he was not right beside us doing. There was no sacrifice we made he did not make with us. Whether it was time, sleep, pushing harder or whatever we needed to do, he was right there with us. The other thing I always appreciated was when we were in planning meetings with our team of advisors. We would go back and forth discussing a topic, stance on an issue or strategy planning. Yemi would always sit back, listen, sort through all the points and then come in and say, "What I'm hearing from everyone is...." And we would then sort and work through all the points to come to the best conclusion as a team. Then, no matter what the decision, we left the room with a united front. We stood together and never faltered. That takes an immense amount of trust. An immense amount of trust in Yemi, in each other and the intentions that we all had to help create a better city. A city focused on the people. Pride was always left at the door. We all had a very real sense we were servants of the people. We are here to lift their voices and lead this city into a new era. But that mentality comes from the top in a team setting. That mentality came from Yemi.

Practicing trust in each other also is a practice in humility. The trust we had amongst the team was incredible, but one ingredient of our secret sauce was the trust Yemi, Anthony, and I had in each other. Yemi brought me in as his Campaign Manager, a Republican and Anthony Carlson, a Democrat, as our brilliant strategist. Yemi, as an Independent, had the foresight that he needed to bring in opposite sides of the aisle as his closest advisors. I will talk more about our backgrounds, but I will save that for later. We also had an advisory board of some of the most brilliant minds in the city. Our advisory board included industry leaders, nonprofit advocates, business founders, religious leaders, and policy advisors. I have never seen a more diverse group of people come together for a single mission, staying so focused on building a city that truly represents all its residents. There were no agendas, no egos, no ulterior motives, just a simple passion to make the city a better place. They saw hope as a reality and unity as a real possibility. They could see themselves in the citizens and they had felt the same frustrations they had felt. All they wanted to do was fight for a new day in Colorado Springs. Together...as one united city.

Chapter Two

A First Time Campaign Manager

Passion Goes a Long Way

W hat would make a candidate trust someone with no prior political experience to run a campaign that would carry so much weight, break down barriers, and compete against candidates with decades of political experience? And why would anyone in their right mind take on that role? To know the answer to that, you must know Yemi and I. It all boils down to, Yemi and I both love a challenge, and we believe in making change for the better. Both of us came from entrepreneurial pasts. We both founded, consulted for, and helped develop multiple nonprofits across the city—so why not dive into the political world together too? He had never run for political office, and I had never run a campaign! It was perfect! Thank God we had Anthony!

Our story of how we met is funny. In 2018, I started working with the Fire Foundation of Colorado Springs. We had an amazing board of directors who were highly active in the city, and I think among all of us, knew every person in the city! As I would work with this group, I kept hearing the same name popping up in conversation after conversation, Yemi Mobolade. I kept thinking to myself, 'Who is this guy? We run in the same circles, work with the same groups. How have I never met him?' I told myself, 'I have to meet this guy.' If he is as impressive as people say, we are going to do something big together one day. (Little did I know!) For the next year, I made it a goal to try to meet this Yemi guy. How hard could it be? We are in all the same places. After what seemed like forever of never meeting, oh well, we have not crossed paths, so we are not meant to meet. Then, of course, the world fell apart in 2020 and threw everything into a tailspin. You all remember that year in which we shall not speak.

In early 2021, my dear friend and then Colorado Springs Fire Department battalion chief, Jesse Kruckberg, and I were having coffee at this little coffee shop near the old north end of downtown. We have met here multiple times discussing the fire department and Fire Foundation business. While meeting one day, my back was to the door and Jesse says, "Oh, my buddy just walked in. You have to meet him." And wouldn't you not know it, it was Mr. Yemi Mobolade! I chuckled and said, "Well, I'll be." I did not know that I should have asked Jesse the whole time to introduce us! And little did I know that the coffee shop we frequented for our meetings was owned by none other than Yemi! It was one of the small businesses that Yemi owned along with Good Neighbor's Meeting House. Be sure to check it out if you are ever in town. There is a reason they call Colorado Springs "Small-orado Springs."

We say that we are a big, small town. That everyone knows everyone and that you only have a couple of degrees of separation from everyone in the city. So, I was thrilled when Jesse finally introduced me to Yemi. And as they say, the rest is history. That day it took us approximately 5 minutes to connect on a multitude of levels, become friends and decide we were going to do big things together. But even though we jumped right in on connecting, I still did not know we would make history just a couple of years later.

Yemi and I immediately got to work on things we wanted to do together. He recruited me to serve on a committee he had formed at the city called COSSBA - Colorado Springs for Small Business Advancement. Yemi was working for the City of Colorado Springs as the Small Business Administrator and I, too, was a small business owner. Not only had my family owned a couple of auto related businesses over the years, but my mother and I owned Day Lily Salon and Spa for 12 years in Colorado Springs. The committee Yemi had formed brought together every government entity that a small business owner had to touch to start and grow their business. This group would all come under one roof for the purpose of removing roadblocks for small business owners and offer them simplified road maps for how to engage and work with these entities. He said I want to bring more small business owners to the table to help us expand our knowledge base of industries, discover their pain points and work out ways to help. They already had a couple of folks on the team, but he wanted more voices at the table. Sound familiar?

I had already built a career in the city as not only a small business owner but also as an advocate for small businesses. Besides my work in the private sector, I also had a stronghold in the nonprofit sector. I have built two parallel careers through my work in both sectors. I had worked in multiple different nonprofits in town to develop, build and expand their sustainable fund development programs and was integrating those two sectors into one through more of a social impact model for for-profit entities. I had been working on my own projects at the time to bring education, training, and exposure to the small business sector. I had developed a local networking events system called *Community and Cocktails* where we brought entrepreneurs together and had a plethora of speakers come in to talk about any topic from startups to scaling, exit planning and more. Yemi and I even participated in one of our panels together with our friend Todd Baldwin, owner of Red Leg Brewing. We wanted to bring these speakers and topics to the business owners instead of always having them seek them out themselves. Think of it as concierge coaching (which inadvertently is the name of my coaching business, *Cicak Concierge Coaching*). I had built a network of owners who needed more support, community, advocacy, and resources. Our focus was to bring speakers in on topics we knew most business owners may not even know they need to educate themselves on. We also asked them what topics they wanted covered, and we went out and found the experts and brought them in to present to the group.

By this point, I had also published my first two books; *Thriving in Salon Ownership: What They Don't Teach You About Owning a Salon* and a children's book I had done with my sister and mom called *Keeping Promises*. I had started speaking at business engagements and seminars on how to thrive in small business ownership. Yemi's interest obviously peaked at the work I was doing and vice versa. It was a match made in heaven. Together, we could help unite the private, nonprofit, and government sectors with the sole purpose of easing the burdens of business ownership, providing education, and building a supportive community.

Yemi and I went straight to work. I integrated into COSSBA, which already had an incredible team established, and we worked to make real change for the city's small business community. One project we worked on was one Yemi spearheaded, called *Permit Partner*. *Permit Partner* acted like a shopping cart potential brick and mortar business could use to go through the process of understanding what permits they would need to open a business. It would also list the government entities the owner needs to reach out to in order to start the processes necessary to acquire said permitting. Think Turbo Tax for permitting. Through the site, we can ask a variety of questions to the owner, in "human speak" and not "code verbiage," to prompt them through the series of questions to help pre-determine which permits they might look to acquire. This would culminate at the end with a ballpark price and a list of what would be needed through the city and could even help have a more accurate number for start-up costs. This program gives the owner a great jumping off point to figure costs and what places they need, from the city side, to get their business open. That committee is still working today to help make it easier for small businesses to do business in the city. Working on that project together was truly a joy. I am still on the COSSBA team today because it puts me right where I want to be to help advocate for the city's small business owners.

One project led to another, and soon he was speaking at my events. We were making connections for a multitude of different networks and making a real impact in the community. But we were just getting warmed up. About another year had gone by and Yemi and I ran into each other at that little coffee shop, his coffee shop. I told him I wanted to chat with him about potential opportunities on the horizon I was investigating and would love his input. He said, "Well, I have one I would like to chat with you about as well. I want to run for mayor." My immediate response was, "You're crazy, but can I vote today!" He said, "I am going to need your help. Are you in?" The resounding YES could not come out of my mouth fast enough. I had no idea what that would entail, but I knew we would figure it out.

Patriotic Roots

Telling my family was the funny part. When I told them Yemi wanted to run for mayor, they were all so excited. Their reactions were priceless. He will be a great mayor, they all said. He is exactly what the city needs. Now the second part was the funny part. I come from a long line of *passionate* people. Some people say fireballs; I prefer to say passionate. My grandfather served as a marine in Guadalcanal. He was one of six siblings. His sister, my great aunt, served in the Women's Army Corp and his brother, my great uncle, was a POW twice while serving in the Army. My grandmother, his wife, was in the Coast Guard. My father was in the Army during Vietnam. To say the least, we Cicak's are passionate and patriotic to the core. Our blood runs red, white, and blue. My family has always believed in serving our country. We believe in fighting for those who cannot fight for themselves. But most of all, we believe in getting involved and educating ourselves on the candidates and issues facing our world. Our motto has always been, *if you do not like what is going on, get off your butt and do something about it.* And more importantly, *you do not get to gripe if you do not get out and vote.* We vote in every election no matter how big or small. We educate ourselves politically so that we can make a truly informed decision. We are involved, to say the least. BUT, as involved as I always was, I swore I would never actively seek taking part in politics. I had all the reasons; it is such a mess now, it is too corrupt, it is this, it is that. Maybe it was just a good old-fashioned rebellion against generations of my family. Who knows? But I have always found it interesting when you hear that little voice from God saying, 'The time is now.' It is important to listen to that voice. I also heard the voice of my family saying, "We need good people doing good, to fix the problems." I honestly believe that. Good people need to stand up, get involved and be the agents of change they wish to see.

So, the minute I told my mom, "I'm going to get involved with Yemi's mayoral campaign," she laughed and said, "Well, it's about time. Your grandpa and your dad would be so proud right now." I knew they would be. My grandfather and my dad were my two most favorite men in the world. And boy, am I just like them! A fighter, stubborn (or as I would prefer to say - passionate) but someone who cares deeply about making our communities a better place for all who live there. I knew that joining Yemi's team would be one of the greatest experiences of my life. I was right. I would never trade a single second of the experience I was able to have. And funny enough, I now have an even stronger passion and drive to become more deeply involved in the political landscape so that I, too, can help make a positive impact on my community.

People often say, 'I had a front-row seat to...whatever it was.' I had the opportunity to be on the playing field. To be in the mud, making the plays and helping call the shots. I have never been a person who sat on the sidelines. From owning my business, building development programs, and advocating for the community...on the field is where I love to be. It is where I am most comfortable. I am not scared of a challenge, in fact, I like them. It energizes me and gets my blood pumping. I played sports growing up, and I compare the experience of politics to playing sports. There is no experience like standing on a field, your chest breathing hard from adrenaline, sweat rolling down your forehead, the smell of the grass, the pain in your body or even the blood running from whatever cut or scrape you just got making the play. The feeling of pure exhaustion but pushing through for your team and walking off that field, battered and bruised...holding the victory trophy.

The Hammer

During the campaign, I lovingly got nicknamed "The Hammer." I love that nickname! As a campaign manager, you become the human shield for your candidate in many ways. We had a situation in the runoff where I had to establish fixed rules, even with the opposing candidate, to set some boundaries around runoff debates. The number of ones that we had done in the general was excessive, to say the least. When it came time for the runoff, I knew there was not enough time to repeat the number that had been done in the general. So, I called the opposing candidates' campaign manager and said, "You and I have to be on the same page with this and set ground rules, that if not followed, we mutually agree not to do the debate." The rules were simple: you must collaborate with other organizations, the debate is no more than 1 hour, and a trained member of the media must be the moderator. If we had not set boundaries around the events, they tended to get a little out of hand. I was not everyone's favorite person when I set ground rules around how they would be conducted. But I knew that to maintain the integrity of the race, respect for the candidates, and the efficiency of the events, we had to rein them in. Sometimes you must bring down the hammer to get things done.

Yemi is one of the kindest and most giving people I know. He wants to give and give to people, and sometimes I would have to help draw boundaries to protect his time, and his mental and physical energy. As a campaign manager, sometimes you must be the "bad guy," and be ok with it. You must set boundaries with the media, all the special requests, along with being the organizer of all things. The cold fact is that there are only 24 hours in a day, and he has a young family at home. Sometimes I had to be the person to "ease" him out of the room or decide what we could or could not attend. But I had to make sure nothing stopped moving, no matter the situation at the time. During the campaign, my family suffered a tragic loss, and I knew that no matter what, we could not miss a single beat, if I had to leave for a short time. Whatever the "rules" or boundaries I had put in place, the team knew that the intention was always for the greater good and the efficiency of the campaign. I never had to worry that they would follow through with whatever task I had set forth because they understood the goal. My goal was always the relentless pursuit of justice, protection for Yemi, my team and the campaign, and doing the right thing. I have always been a passionate fighter for justice and for those that cannot fight for themselves. I believe in healthy boundaries, clear and concise direction and making sure that no matter what craziness was happening around us, we never lost pursuit of the mission. That our northern star stayed at the center of our focus, and we never veered from the path.

The greatest lessons I have learned in my career are that you can be firm but fair. You can say no with grace. You must lead with dignity and strength because your team needs you to. You must listen and be humble, but when you need to stand firm, you cannot waiver. Be grounded in your values and know when there is a time to bend and time to dig your heels in. But none of these things you do can be done without love and a base built on trust. When you must be the rock, you must be strong enough to not break. Others in your life will lean on you in ways you cannot imagine. When they need to break down, you know you are strong enough to pick them back up, help them brush off and turn back to the battlefield together. Trust me when I say that I had my moments and my circle I went to when I needed a minute. But when you are where the buck stops, you must be consistent, fair, and resilient. You cannot waiver in your pursuit of leadership and the direction of your team. I can totally see where I got the nickname "The Hammer" and know that I wear that nickname as the greatest badge of honor ever given to me.

Chapter Three

Inspiration Won the Day

The Ground Swell

I nspiration won the day! These were the words spoken by the editor of the Colorado Springs Gazette after Yemi Mobolade secured his spot in the mayoral runoff election in April 2023. And he was right. We had won the general election by quite a decent margin for a field of twelve candidates. Yes, you read that right—twelve candidates—to advance us to the runoff. Many people doubted we could do it. 'We like him; he is a really nice guy. But he does not have a snowball's chance in this town,' was the sentiment we often heard from those who could not envision a path to victory. "There is no way an independent wins in this city. People are not ready for a West African immigrant here. He has never run for political office before. Good luck, but there is just no way." We were eager to prove that this city was, indeed, ready and hungry for something different, for someone different.

Inspiration is an interesting concept. It is defined as the process that occurs when someone sees or hears something that sparks new ideas or prompts them to take action. I believe this city has long awaited someone not just to inspire them, but to give them hope. Hope that the city could be different. That it could rise above the past, opening hearts and minds to new ideas, new ways of thinking, and the realization that politics did not have to be business as usual. People were reminded that they have a voice, and that voice deserves to be heard. We showed them that not only was someone listening, but that someone was standing at the helm ready to act on their behalf. Someone who had THEIR best interests at heart. There was a pervasive sense that the 'status quo' would always prevail, and that the voices of the people had been drowned out by the day-to-day operations of running a city and maintaining the same old ways.

And then Yemi Mobolade arrived

People did not expect the spark he would ignite within them. They did not anticipate feeling what they felt. To know Yemi, is to love Yemi. As a campaign manager, I used to tell the team, "All I have to do is get him in a room with someone and he does the rest." Once he explained his "why" and what this city meant to him, they got it. One citizen told me that while he knew they did not agree on every issue, he was going to vote for him because he was the only candidate who truly 'heard' him. "I trust he will hear all sides and do his best to make a decision that is best for all of us," was what he told me. He will find the middle ground. Where had we lost that in politics? Why had we lost that? I think those in the political landscape have stopped listening or they are too consumed with re-elections and making sure the groups in power stay happy. People told me throughout the campaign that they had not felt heard by politicians in decades. That the city/county/state/nation is just going to do whatever it does, and we must hold on. That their government was not accessible, and it felt that it only had its own interests in mind.

There was this incredible experience that we had while on the campaign trail. We met with thousands of residents at over 110 meet and greets. We knocked on over 40,000 doors and kept hearing the same comments again and again. "We're fed up" was the underlying theme of most Colorado Springs citizens. We are fed up with the division, the fighting, not being heard and not having our needs and opinions considered. They were leaving their parties left and right—pun intended! People would tell us they were on their way out of the city because they just could not take it anymore. Decades of irresponsible growth had severely impacted infrastructure, and the cost of living was spiraling out of control. Wages were not keeping up with the cost of living. High-paying jobs were scarce, and those that did exist required specialties not reflected in the city's workforce. What motivation did they have to stay? We were also told that people felt DC politics had trickled down to our city and that national problems were overflowing into our town and someone had to bring unity. And no one in power was addressing it. More importantly, they were not listening to the concerns of the constituents.

People want to discuss it! They want a platform where the community can have an open dialogue with city leadership (and let us be honest; they want it to the highest office in the nation) to discuss their concerns. We also found that they want to get involved and help find the solutions. But no one is opening that door of communication to constituents. We would say, 'We are not going to govern AT you; we want to govern WITH you. That whole "a government by the people and for the people" thing, crazy I know! The major pain points we encountered with the community was that they are fed up with the division. They are tired of being used as pawns in political games. The truth of the matter is that most people float somewhere in the middle of most issues. They are not hardcore far right or left. Voter patterns in Colorado Springs show that the largest growing "party" is unaffiliated! The divisiveness stemming from DC politics does not represent the everyday American. Are there extremists out there? Absolutely, but they are the minority, not the majority. The beautiful thing is that no one understands the need or has the drive to unite people more than Yemi. Yemi's first goal in any situation is to unite those forces around any issue in a respectful, trustworthy, and action-oriented manner. No matter the office, no matter the role or position, we first must bring people together and work in unison to find the solutions that benefit the community.

A Leader's Leader

His leadership style is truly magnificent to behold. He is first transparent with everyone around him. His humility radiates. He is courageous in his pursuit to unify this city, and he holds space for those with which we need to show empathy. But my favorite part of his leadership style is that he is a man of action. While he accepts you as you are, he cares too much to let you stay there. His ability to absorb information, process it and start forming an action plan makes him the leader he has become. His mind immediately shifts to action, brainstorming who needs to be brought to the table for problem-solving, and then he dives into the action items needed to pursue that goal. He is aware of his own weaknesses and is not afraid to express them. He pulls people into the room who are strong and well versed in an area where he is not, so he can have all the best tools in the problem-solving toolbox. That requires humility. He is not intimidated by someone who knows more than him on a subject, instead he pulls out a chair and says, "Teach me more about that." That takes courage. And when the downtrodden come to him for help, he encourages them and lifts them up. That requires empathy.

When we were at a meet and greet, people came expecting to hear a talk given by Yemi about who he is and all his platform topics and campaign promises. But what they got was Yemi taking a few minutes to welcome everyone, saying a few words, then he would start asking questions. He said, this is not about me. What do you need me to do? What concerns do you have? How can we make this city better for you and your families, together? He simply listened. He rarely said much at meet and greets. He provided a platform where residents could tell him how they feel. What they want for the city. You know what we heard a lot…I want a city my kids want and can afford to come back to. Whoa. It does not matter how great a city is or what people think of it if the residents are not experiencing it themselves. We had to get that back. We had to breathe new life into the city.

What we saw happening from these conversations was this intense ground swell. Meet and greets started getting bigger and bigger. People were answering and engaging with us at their doors. They all started signing up to volunteer. Everybody and their brother wanted yard signs! We could hardly keep up with the demand for yard signs or find enough places for volunteers! What a great problem to have! People could see this bright future for Colorado Springs, and they believed a city for the many, was an achievable goal.

The Effect

I am convinced it all happened because Yemi was listening. I have never met a candidate who listens as genuinely as he does. He made himself accessible and approachable. That had not been the experience most people had in the city prior to him coming on the scene. Yemi is a person of action, and he never stops. He gathered and gathered information, resources, and before we even won, started getting to work on correcting the problems people were expressing. He lit a path forward for action, unity, and results.

Unity was the Focus

He ran on a platform of unity, aiming to bridge the deep divide in this country. Division that had ruled elections at all levels for decades. He ran on a platform that disrupted the status quo. And boy, did it disrupt it! He ran as an independent, in a city that had a long history of conservative candidates, for a seat that had been held by republicans for longer than I can remember. Now, in Colorado Springs, the mayoral seat is a non-partisan seat. But it has always been discussed, as to the political affiliation of the candidate. But in every conversation when people would ask, we would tell them, "This is a non-partisan seat, and he is unaffiliated." People's minds were blown. This is a seat that must remain neutral. Also, Colorado Springs had never elected an African American mayor before. We disrupted everything people thought they knew here.

I always feel like Susan Pattee, one of our campaign advisors, summed up the feelings of voters across the city best when she said, "I have never been more excited for anything in my life!" Supporters told us they had this vision for the city that was unlike anything we had seen prior. That there was truly a new day on the horizon. Thomas Thompson, our co-board chair, said, "I have never gotten involved in politics because I felt like it never mattered. The national stage made it feel like it did not matter. But with Yemi, I want to get deeply involved because I feel like I can make a difference. And we get to mold the Colorado Springs we want to see for our grandkids." He felt like we helped create an identity for our future. Mike Juran, CEO of Altia, co-chair of the board said to me he felt like people realized what being bipartisan meant. "Being a part of this campaign, it's like everyone forgot why they are so stuck on being liberal or conservative. They just want their life to be better." He said, 'The formula for happiness is:'

- Good relationships

- Good family life

- Good social life

- Good community

We can help with at least one of those." And he is right. Most voters just want their lives to be better. The fighting does not motivate them, especially when someone has to be right. They want to know that their leaders have a plan, and they are working for the better of the community. It is like Thomas Thompson said, "The people were asked, who is going to write the story of our city? Because what they wanted was to write their own story."

Chapter Four

The Candidate

Who Is This Yemi

W ho is Yemi Mobolade? He will tell you he is first a husband to his bad ass wife Abbey (and I can attest to the fact that she is a bad ass!), father to three young kids (he will also joke that the struggle is real! Haha!), a pastor, a civil servant and a man who fell in love with America the moment he arrived. On a side note, if you ever meet him, have him tell you about becoming an American citizen. It was one of the happiest days of his life. As a Nigerian exchange student, he arrived in South Bend, Indiana, to stay with family and attend college. He studied, worked, and absorbed everything he could. He knew he was home the minute he arrived in America. He also became a big Notre Dame football fan. To this day, he proudly flies the Notre Dame flag in his front yard during football season, just below the American flag.

Yemi originally came to Colorado Springs to plant a church. He will tell you that when he stepped foot out of the moving truck, he heard God say, "Welcome Home." He quickly fell in love with the city and everything it had to offer. He and Abbey went to work building a church, a family, and a life. Yemi always had an entrepreneurial heart. Not only did he help start a church here, but he also started three small businesses. Two of these were a response to what he heard from the youth in his church. "We are moving out of Colorado Springs because there is nothing cool to do here. There are no cool spots to just go hang out." So Yemi said, I can help fix that problem. He opened two different coffee and meeting house spaces where people could just go hang out. He created a cultural spot where college kids could sit and do homework, where church groups could meet for bible studies and busy professionals could host meetings and grab a bite to eat. He wanted to create a space that not only generated jobs but also fostered culture in the city. His work and the respect he garnered in the nonprofit and small business community led him to eventually become the Small Business Administrator for the City of Colorado Springs. There, he found the perfect platform to support, build up, and facilitate small business growth.

Yemi is a visionary. He has the drive, foresight, and leadership to not only spot a need or gap in whatever project he might work on, but he takes action to fill it. He builds his circle wide because he believes in the power of people and their ability to rise to meet a challenge. He has a way of activating those people around him and plugging them in to exactly the best place for them to shine, thrive and flourish. He has a unique ability to see people's potential and place them in just the right role to solve problems or expand projects. People line up to follow him because they know he will lead them to get sh*t done! They know that with Yemi at the helm, there will be structure, action, and a focus on the greater good. They see something in themselves. It is like when you work with Yemi, you somehow see your own potential and abilities differently because he does. He inspires you to push harder, to stretch your own skills, and he pushes you to a place of greatness you may not have even known you possess. It is like he fosters this thing inside you that helps you believe you can accomplish anything. He will always be in your corner, and he will always strive to be your biggest cheerleader. Who would not want to follow or work with someone who brings out the best in you?

Great leaders are a rare commodity in the world today. It takes an incredibly special person to foster your ability to create your own greatness. Mike Juran told me that one of his favorite aspects of this campaign was the opportunity it provided for us to shape our city's destiny. That the people themselves could create that destiny through Yemi's leadership. We finally had a candidate and a platform where we could take real action to create this "shining city on a hill" as we would say. He said for the first time he felt like he, as an everyday citizen, could help write the future for his city. The relationships built and fostered through this process were priceless, proving that everyday people can have a say in how our city grows. Mike said, "This is my town. My family's home. This is the meeting place for the people I love. And I want to be proud of this city." He is proud now. He shines every time we discuss Yemi and what he is doing for the city. He discussed his daughter's wedding like a proud Papa and told me he brought their entire family from around the world here, to this city, to celebrate. The city he proudly calls home.

A Family Man Through and Through

Abbey, his beautiful wife, tells people that when she married Yemi, she took his hand and jumped! And they have been jumping ever since! But that's Yemi, never afraid of the next adventure. He may have a few bruises and scars, but they have only driven him to become better.

When he told his parents and siblings that he was going to run for mayor, the entire family's response was, it was about time! They had always known that he would serve his community in some big way. Yemi not only has a passion for serving his community, but he wants to show his children that they can do remarkable things. If you work hard and you love people, you can accomplish any dream you set your mind to. He wants his kids to recognize the opportunities this country offers and understand what it means to be an American citizen. He wants them to see their own potential and to have the courage to chase their dreams.

Staying Grounded

I am not sure I have ever met anyone who has a greater capacity to stay grounded. Yemi has the discipline to drown out the noise around him, not just during the campaign, but even now. He drowns out the media surrounding him. Whether it be the naysayers or those giving the atta boys...he does not absorb it. He does not want to be distracted by either. He stays focused on the job at hand. Whether people's opinions of him are good or bad, it does not matter to him. What matters is being focused on the job and staying the course.

Even when it becomes a partisan issue, his philosophy stays the same. There will be noise coming at him from both sides, and he has an innate ability to stay focused on nothing more than the core fundamental issue at hand. It does not matter who is pushing their agenda; what matters is what is best for the people.

I think the thing I appreciate him the most for is his ability to humanize politics. He never loses sight of the fact that those who oppose him are still human beings who, despite their disagreements, deserve basic human dignity. That they too are a child of God and that we can still be respectful. Seems like something we all learned as children but cannot seem to practice as adults!

When you have a field of twelve candidates at a debate or forum, things get interesting quickly. You can see the worst or the best in people. You would witness character attacks, people tearing each other down, and blatant disrespect for fellow human beings. And then you would see Yemi step forward as the example of how it "can be." When the candidates were asked a question, Yemi was the only one who consistently stuck to the issue and answered the question directly. He had a plan. He laid it out and stayed calm, cool, and collected the entire time. He was the only candidate who would pause and listen attentively to the other candidates while they spoke. He acknowledged that it was their time to speak and actively engaged in the discussion. When it came his turn to answer, he answered the question. One of our board members told me he knew during the debates that we would win, because of how Yemi carried himself, stuck to the issues and had a plan to move forward. The way the crowds would respond to him was how he knew. They were engaged, their heads would be nodding, etc. With Yemi, there was no going negative...not once. One of the other candidates mentioned to our team later that Yemi was the only other candidate who showed them dignity during the campaign. After debates, he would shake hands and recognize the other candidates. He understood that even after a victory, he would still need their engagement. Yemi understood the genius of Abraham Lincoln. While we are not on the same side of every issue, the genius behind the *Team of Rivals* makes for a stronger city.

Last, but certainly not least, I believe Yemi's ability to stay focused and grounded stems from his deep-rooted faith. He has a center that cannot be shaken because it is first rooted in God. He practices true genuine Christian love for all people. He sees God in other people, and it is why he has more compassion than most people we encounter. It does not matter if you are black, white, purple, or green, an R or a D, pro-life or pro-choice, straight, or part of the LGBTQ community, a person of faith or not...Yemi will treat you the same. He will love you, embrace you and show you the dignity and respect that you deserve as a human being. He believes it is not his job to judge one way or the other but simply to love his fellow man and that is what being a true leader means.

Chapter Five

I Am Because We Are

The Magic

S poiler alert! Proud mama moments ahead! I will do my best to get through this next section without leaving tear stains on the pages. My team, my team! There are not enough thank you's in the world for what my team accomplished. There comes a moment in everyone's career when all the stars align, and every piece of the puzzle falls perfectly into place. It is the magic you cannot create, but the magic that happens organically. I used to say every day, my team makes me look good. Leading them was one of the greatest honors of my life. The passion, the unrelenting pursuit of the greater good and the sacrifices they made are more than I can ever share. My cup overflows with gratitude.

When I interviewed members of the board and team, we discussed various aspects of the campaign and what was meaningful to them. Story after story, filled with tears of happiness and laughter, came up during those conversations. But when I asked, 'What was your favorite part of the campaign?' the unanimous answer was, 'The team!' Everyone on this team loved, respected, and enjoyed the time they had together. They grew as friends and teammates while being in the trenches of campaigning together. I have never seen a group of people who grew so tight knit so fast. Even today, we laugh when we run into each other in the city. It is like magnets that cannot stay apart. We run to each other and that is where we stay for the rest of the event. It is so beautiful. The camaraderie that is built when you fight for a united mission cannot be beaten.

Each member of this team was a rock star in their own right, but together, they were unstoppable. Every person was a leader in their industry. What they all brought to the table was not only years of experience and community relationships but in-depth knowledge of their respective fields. Most of them had never worked on a campaign before but some had door knocked before. As a collective they had little to no political experience, including me! In a way, that worked to our advantage. The status quo or the mentality of politics as usual had not encumbered them. They had new fresh ideas because they were coming at this, as regular everyday citizens fighting for a cause.

I have never met people with more fire and drive inside of them. If you have never worked on a campaign, you have missed out on truckloads of cold pizza, countless sleepless nights, and the fear that comes with diving headfirst into one of the scariest challenges you have ever faced. There is so much at stake when you take on a role in a campaign. What makes it all bearable—and even fun—is the people standing beside you in the trenches. The people who understand your scars, share inside jokes, and the person you trust to pack your parachute become the family you did not even know you needed. We worked together, celebrated together, and felt sorrow together when we were attacked. We did not have big budgets, but we had plenty of manpower. Every dollar we raised was precious. Together, we embodied what it means to run a grassroots campaign. Even if we never work together again, each of these people will hold a special place in my heart.

Our Strategist

The first person I want to say thank you to is my campaign partner and our political strategist, Anthony Carlson. Anthony, when you read this, I hope you understand the overwhelming amount of gratitude and respect I have for you. I tell people Anthony and I were the perfect political marriage! Haha! We could not have come from more opposite places politically, but always found our common ground and used that to help advise Yemi and drive the mission of the campaign forward. We had a fundamental respect and honor for each other's backgrounds, career accomplishments and the wisdom we both brought to the table in our respective roles. There was no competition, no pride, no egos. Just the core united mission of making this city the best it could be.

We believed in Yemi, this city, our team and each other. We had a healthy and respectful way of dealing with conflict. If we did not agree completely on a way to move forward, we talked it out. We talked through all the scenarios and pulled the pros and cons forward to come to a symbiotic resolution. I would joke and say, when mom and dad walk out these doors, we must be a united front! We must be on the same page for the team.

Mike Juran told us we worked so well together because Anthony was the strategy, and I was the implementation. When Mike and Yemi met Anthony, Mike said, "I'll only do this if Anthony is involved. He's the guy that can help us win." He was right. Their initial conversation was where my name came to step in as Campaign Manager. Mike said that now all the pieces were in place. Anthony was the strategy, Yemi was the product, and I was the execution. Together we reached critical mass. The chain reaction to a win had been set in motion.

When Anthony and I first met, I was like...yes, this is the guy. He had come from several winning campaigns. He had a great reputation in town. The man is a political savant! The wealth of knowledge and experience that guy holds in his head is awe-inspiring. There were so many things I appreciated about him. We both agreed on how we wanted to run this campaign. We wanted to change the usual cast of characters in the local political scene, and we wanted to empower the citizens to take part in their local politics. We wanted to disrupt partisan politics. It was the perfect race to do it in since the mayor's seat is a non-partisan seat and people needed to be reminded of that. We could not allow party politics to creep in. Having an independent candidate was the first way we could push back on that mindset.

Watching Anthony work is a magical thing. He is a workhorse like no other. His ability to think through a problem, to focus and get creative with solutions is part of what makes him as successful as he is. When you do not have big money funneled into your campaign, you get highly creative and strategic on the best ways to spend what you have. We would joke that he would spend it, and I would go raise it! Thank God we had the fundraising team we did! But what I admire most about him is his passion for the work. He genuinely believes in what is *possible*. He has a huge heart, and he wants to empower people to be the change in their communities. He wants to help shepherd the process for change along. I think secretly, deep inside, he is an idealist. While he is an absolute machine at the practical, what lies underneath all that is a visionary.

The Power of People Participating

They said we were young, that our team did not have the political experience necessary to win an election like this. But they turned out to be the dream team. I called them the hardest-working team in politics. We had the best of the best! And they were all volunteers! I had the esteemed pleasure of leading a team of leaders. We had eight teams with over one hundred volunteers in total, and they were the reason for our success. They had other jobs, families, and commitments, and yet they found the time to give this campaign everything they had. Long hours, no sleep, more cheese and cracker trays than you would ever want to eat, and they did it with a smile. I could write a novel about each member of our team and what made them unique and magical in their own way. Every single person on this campaign played a vital role in the success of this charge. From Yemi all the way through our field team and every position in and around it, every single person's work mattered. They sacrificed time with their families to volunteer for what many called an underdog campaign. And they did it with a smile and more vigor than you could ever externally ignite in people. Their energy level throughout the year was awe-inspiring! Joining a campaign is a deeply personal commitment. You cannot do this kind of work FOR just anybody, but anybody CAN do this work and that is what our campaign team exemplified.

The Incomparable Joe Hollmann, Chair of Communications

Every sector of our team had a shining star. Our Chair of Communications, Joe Hollmann, was one of those bright shining lights. His ability, along with his team's, to take data and translate it into accessible information is a rare gift. His story telling ability, his creativity, and his ability to showcase and highlight the best in people was a thing of beauty. The communication strategies he helped implement made our campaign approachable, effective, and welcoming. And we figured out how to do it on a shoestring budget. My favorite story to tell about Joe was the day he came to Anthony and said, "I have an idea." First, for any of you who may not know, campaign finance reports are public information. You can comb through any of that data and learn anything you want to know about who is financing campaigns. Now, good luck finding it and good luck trying to translate and break it down into something that makes sense. Joe said, "What if we take all that data and translate it into consumable information? What if we tell the story through charts and graphs? The data becomes transparent and there is a story that is easy to tell and understand." Anthony said run with it! Game Changer! The minute we released the campaign finance reports in the new easy-to-read format, the media jumped all over it! It was brilliant. The story was being told. More importantly, the public could easily consume the information, making informed decisions about campaign funding. We were asked over and over what big time political marketing firm we had hired to do our communications. We did not need a "big time" firm, we had the brilliance of Joe Hollmann. There were two major factors in our win: our communications, and our field program.

The Ground Game

People are still discussing our ground game. We had one of the most brilliant, hardworking, organized, goddess of a Field Organizer in Ms. Abbi Groft-Kelly. I do not know what I would have done without Abbi. She is one of the greatest leaders I have seen emerge in my career. She organized about 100 volunteers working mostly on the weekends (in the snowiest months of the year in Colorado) to knock 40,000+ doors over the course of approximately 5 months. It was one of the most well-oiled machines I had ever seen in action. We canvassed every section of town; we had a clean and organized supply chain of materials that never ran out, along with plans for getting people yard signs while we were in the field. Let me tell you, our yard sign game was strong! But our field game was unmatched! I credit a huge part of our win to our door knocking program. People lined up to volunteer and help out. Everyday citizens (not paid canvassers) who would tell us over and over that they had done nothing like this before. They had never volunteered for a campaign, never donated, and some of them had never even voted before! But that all changed with this campaign. They got out in the snow and the cold with their thermoses of hot cocoa and coffee, all bundled up to spread the news because they understood a vote for Yemi meant a vote for Colorado Springs. Even my 16-year-old niece joined Yemi and me in door-knocking. She told me how much she loved Yemi, and she wanted to learn about her civic responsibilities. Let me tell you what that did for this auntie's heart!

Devoted volunteers, willing to learn, brought a fiery passion to ensure that every ear in Colorado Springs heard Yemi's name. Abbi's ability to hone that excitement and fervor into constructive and effective advocacy was an unparalleled feat of leadership. I will forever be indebted to Abbi for what she and her fearless team of door knockers accomplished.

Each of the 100+ people who worked on this campaign made an impact. From Tariro "T" Chibodo and Yemi (yes, we had two Yemi's!) Sanchez for being the two people it took to keep me and Yemi organized, to Niki Fields and Jenn Cancellier helping with volunteer coordination and events, to Jenn Strehlow who organized all our thank-you card writing volunteers, to Isaac Norton who mastered our newsletter communications, to the entire communications team, to my dear friend Susan Pattee who was my right hand in fundraising, Mike Juran, Thomas Thompson, Vance Brown and our exceptional advisory board and the countless others who made this dream a reality, thank you from the bottom of my heart. YOU made this all possible, and I celebrate our win with you every day.

In Yemi's words.... "I am because we are."

Chapter Six

Stories From the Campaign Trail

What Yemi Inspired

I have told you about the team, but what about the city? The stories of why citizens got involved would pull at your heartstrings. The stories of kids who wanted to get involved because their parents were, and the overwhelming number of people who told me, 'I have never done this before, but I want to help,' were astonishing. I cannot tell you how many people told me they had never volunteered on a campaign before, never even put a yard sign out, much less door knocked. People who had never donated to campaigns before were not only donating what they could but rallying support from friends and family to do the same. We have talked about the groundswell, but until you have seen it in person, words cannot fully capture it.

I had never seen or experienced anything like it before. People were coming out of the woodwork asking what they could do to help. We had to assign a person to do nothing but coordinate volunteers, besides the person who was running our field team! People felt like they were part of something bigger than themselves and the coolest part...it was people from both sides of the aisle, from every walk of life and every background you could imagine. Republicans, Democrats, and everyone in between would sit together, discussing issues from opposite sides, yet engaging in respectful, inquisitive dialogue. The way it was meant to be, the way it CAN be. Everyone knew this was a safe space to have open conversation because that was the culture we were creating. People knew that if they voted for Yemi, that level of respect, open dialogue and active listening would continue into the mayor's office.

The Youth

As a proud Gen Xer myself, I can now say I am old enough to discuss *those young ins,* as we say in the south. Every generation has worries and concerns about the generation behind them. I can tell you firsthand the concerns my grandparents and parents had about mine, and I have expressed concerns about the ones behind me. But I am here to tell you, there is hope. The engagement that we had from our youth was overwhelming! I want to give a shout out to all the parents that got their kids involved. Teaching your children about their civic responsibilities and RIGHTS is crucial. An important thing. And must be continued. Remember when I told you earlier about my grandfather and my parents and all they taught me about our government and our civic duty? I am the product of what that looks like in adulthood. The younger generations learn nothing until we TEACH them. If there is no greater call to action than this, teach your children about the country they live in, with pride. If you do not feel knowledgeable in an area, then learn TOGETHER. Every person should take Civics, Advanced Civics and U.S. History classes, if you ask me. Whoo! Preach! I will now climb down from my soapbox. And you are welcome! But the amount of kids that would show up with their parents at events to help volunteer would make your heart swell.

Teenagers would go door knocking with their parents, not even old enough to vote, but were so inspired by Yemi that they wanted to be involved. I mentioned my niece in the last chapter. She became my wonderful assistant throughout the campaign. She went door knocking with Yemi and I, she would attend meet and greets. She could repeat Yemi's talks herself; she went to so many. What was happening? She was listening and learning. At dinner one night at my sister's house, she and my nephews were discussing the campaign. Yes, I said a high schooler, a middle schooler and an elementary school age little boy were discussing a political campaign. They informed me they had been terribly busy at school telling all their friends that they needed to tell their parents to vote for Yemi! And they were not just flippantly saying, "Vote for Yemi," they were getting into the nitty gritty of the issues with their friends! "That's not exactly how Yemi feels about the homeless crisis. You have that wrong. This is his plan..." Then they would rattle off what they had learned. Best part, it was right! I cried and laughed all at the same time. I knew I had done my job as an aunt and that my parents and grandparents would be proud. One day, my 7-year-old nephew cried in the car. When I asked what was wrong, he said he was not old enough to vote for Yemi. I cried. All. The. Tears. But what got me from that conversation at the dinner table was how emotionally damaged they were by the negative ads being run. It touched them. They would ask me, "Why are they saying those mean things about him? He is not that person. He is a good man and wants to do good things for the city. Why would they lie?" "I don't know, baby," was all I could muster. The moral of that story is that our children are listening. They are being affected by everything that is swirling around them. They are hyper exposed to the "bad things" and way under exposed to the "good things" these days. They are being affected by what we say and what they hear, and the world should be a little more thoughtful about what we are exposing our children to.

We were also told a story about a 17-year-old daughter of one volunteer. While she herself could not vote, she had been going around to all her friends who were old enough to vote, telling them about Yemi. She even helped her friends register to vote! What?! What kid cares about campaigns this much? We heard story after story like this. We even had one of the highest turnouts of young and first-time voters in Colorado Springs.

Stories of Hope

Citizens would approach me with big smiles and say, 'I am just so happy! I have hope for the future of the city! I do not know about you, but prior to Yemi's race, I cannot remember the last time I felt hopeful about any election. And hope swarmed all around us. It fueled us like fire. We used it to stay strong, focused and push harder and harder. I have been registered to vote since as soon as I turned 18 years old. I was forty-four at the time of the election. The day I took my ballot to the box, I sat in my car, and I cried. I was so overwhelmed with emotion. For the first time in my life, I GOT to vote for the RIGHT candidate, the BEST candidate. I did not have to vote for the lesser of two evils we all discuss. I got to vote for the person I know who cares about the city. Who cares about its residents and will immediately get to work bringing unity. He will disrupt the status quo and partisan antics. For the first time, I got to vote for the right guy.

People told me over and over they had the same experience when casting their ballots. Yemi and our team proved it does not have to be the way it has always been. This election became something so much bigger than a local mayoral election. You could see something clear at last—people were brightening again. They said, we now see this is possible, that this can be done in other places and that this type of campaign and political practice CAN exist. People from across the country began watching and following what was happening in Colorado Springs. Higher levels of government paid attention. We rattled cages—and it was about time. People would say they realized that we all need to get more involved and educate ourselves on how we can make a difference in our communities. Because it all starts locally.

The Awakening

The number of people who told me they only voted in federal elections, if at all, before this election was astonishing. It downright broke my patriotic heart. They said, "But that changes today." I stressed to people over and over that every single election is important. That men and women have laid their lives down to protect our right to vote. That we need to exercise that right every single chance we get. Local elections are especially important because they most directly affect your day-to-day living. Of course, county, state and federal elections are vitally important as well, but you can create real change for your day-to-day life in local elections. BUT...do not be flippant about casting your vote. Educate yourself on the candidates and the ballot issues. Dig into them and learn the nuances of each. Vote for what you believe aligns with your values. I hate it when we feel like we have to vote against something rather than for something. And for heaven's sake, do not vote for or against someone's skin color, or gender, or because you like the way someone dresses. You might laugh. But I have heard them all. Someone told me, well I just voted for the girl in that election. I almost died. Someone else told me once they voted for the "guy on the end" because they liked the way he dressed. People! Come on now! My reply was, "Do you know if this person's values align with your values at all? Do you know where they land on the issues? And is that in agreement with how you feel about them?" It is then that I get the deer in the headlights look. But if we proved nothing else, it is that when people are awakened to the power of possibility, it completely changes their mindset on how they vote.

Voting is one of the most sacred rights we hold as Americans. So many countries' citizens do not have the rights that we have. They do not have any power or voice in how they are governed. Voting is how we choose the people who will represent us. It is how we put our voice forward in issues that affect our lives. Do not make those decisions lightly and do not take it for granted. And if you cannot find a name on a ballot you want to support...it should be your name on that ballot. Who knows? But if you want to see change, the beauty of this country is that you have the power to make it happen. Get involved! Everyday citizens founded this country, and they are still the people who should lead it.

Stories of Faith

I want to take a moment and discuss my experiences of faith on this journey. Yemi and I are both people of faith. In fact, sometimes just he and I would stop and say a prayer when we needed a little grounding or strength. Neither of us believes that our personal experiences need to be forced on anyone else. That is our journey, but an important one for us, nonetheless. There were two moments for me during the campaign where I saw him shine in that role. People often ask me when I knew we were going to win, and these two stories are when I knew. A few months before the election, an issue arose in the city and we knew as a candidate there was a possibility that they may ask the running candidates for quotes, "Well if you were the mayor now, how would you handle this scenario?" So, we prepared statements and made sure Yemi had both sides of the story and so on. While we were briefing him, he went to Anthony and me, and requested our opinions. Anthony advised him on what the democrat constituency will feel. Then he called me, and I explained from the republican perspective. Then I asked him, "But how do you feel about it, Yemi?" He sat there for a minute, and he said, "It doesn't matter how I feel. I need to think about how Jesus would handle this. He would not care about the sides of the aisle. I think he would want to protect people from harm but also protect the citizens of this city. That's what I have to do." I stopped dead in my tracks and thought, "Oh yeah! Of course." And we found the middle.

The second story is one that still makes me emotional. The morning before election night, a group of friends, mentors, and pastors, came together with Yemi and Abbey and we prayed. We gathered with them as friends in faith, along with their family. We prayed for their strength and wisdom for Yemi. But we prayed that no matter how the night ended, win, or lose, that God's will be done. That if it was not Yemi's time that we had faith in that God had a better plan at play. It was the most moving and peaceful moment of the entire campaign. Few people can say they felt calm and peaceful on the morning of an election. As I got in my car and sat there, I knew. I just knew. And I thought, "We better be ready. This is happening."

Chapter Seven

The Game Plan

Positivity, Accountability and Unity

An unconventional candidate cannot run a conventional campaign—wise words from Anthony. This became our unspoken motto. We wanted to break the status quo, and that starts with how you campaign. When Yemi and I first discussed me coming on, I told him I wanted to finish this with my dignity and integrity intact and I knew he of course wanted the same thing for all of us. Citizens have complained for years about the mudslinging that occurs during campaign cycles and how disgusted they feel when they see it on TV or receive a mailer. But this is just politics, someone said to us. Yemi and I made a commitment that at no point in this process would we go negative. We held on to that to the very end. Every message would be positive. We did not care what any other candidate did or said. We would stick to our issues and promote our message. If you focus on telling people where you stand and what you plan to do in office, rather than worrying about what others are saying, people will trust you and your purpose. Yemi was adamant about being a clear voice amongst the chaos. Our goal was radical positivity.

When Yemi was on debate stages, which was always quite interesting with twelve candidates, no matter the chaos that would ensue on the stage, he stayed the course of positivity. He stuck to discussing his policies when answering questions. He stayed out of the weeds of everything else. Paving a new road in the middle of an already established landscape is always tough. You must fight harder to stay focused and be resilient, as that landscape will fight to keep you in its original form. Staying grounded and mission-focused is how you disrupt that landscape.

Day after day after day, people would bend over backwards to thank us for staying positive. A few people said, "Seeing you being attacked the way you are and yet not one negative word about anyone else ever came out of this campaign's messaging is extraordinary. On behalf of all us citizens, thank you. "You have my vote." People wanted something they could believe in and someone they could get behind, not just a vote *against* someone else. Contrast emerges naturally when you give people something to believe in. We never had to fight to contrast ourselves from other people. It happened organically. The community recognized that Yemi Mobolade was a different candidate, not just for what we did, but for what we did not do. Susan Pattee said it best when she commented, "He never once got caught up in the swirl of the attacks. He just moved on past it." When they saw this, you could watch the local community influencers line up behind him. They started telling their networks and then it was like watching a wildfire grow. I think the fact that this was such a grassroots movement was not what the other sides expected. The other camps just assumed they would win. They did not see what was happening until it was so big that it could not be stopped. The community had spoken, and it spoke out in a roar. Mike Juran said, "You do not know someone until you know them in adversity." Yemi showed brighter than ever in the face of adversity.

The TV Ads

The place I loved our messaging the most was our campaign TV ads. They were my favorite. I am a person who loves a good story, and we got to tell beautiful visual stories in our ads. Some of my favorite ones you can still find on YouTube. There was one where Yemi and Abbey are playing games with the kids on the floor and Yemi discusses what is at stake for our families in Colorado Springs. We had one where Abbey discussed what some of the issues we face mean to her as both a mom and a nurse. We used to call Abbey our secret weapon! She is so lovable and approachable. She and Yemi are raising three children in the city. Their story is similar to that of thousands of families in the city. The same issues we face with public safety, housing costs and neighborhood growth affect them just the same. But my all-time favorite ad was an idea Anthony had, to do a nod to Ronald Reagan's *It's Morning Again in America* presidential ad, he ran during his reelection campaign. We called it *A New Day in Colorado Springs*. We highlighted local families and how we can create a city where families can thrive. The best part was we used everyday families and not actors. We used real families, including my friend and her daughter and my mom and nephew, amongst others. We wanted it to be real life. We wanted to highlight what real families are doing each day. You should check it out—I still get a little teary-eyed when I watch it.

Another one that I still love was our *Road to the Runoff* ad. It dropped as soon as we went from the general election to the runoff. In the ad Yemi thanks everyone who voted for him and tells those who did not vote that he hopes to earn your vote. It was so important to us to make sure and say thank you. There were so many people doing so much to help and for everyone who cast a ballot with Yemi's name, we wanted to express our gratitude. It also helped let folks know that the election was not over and that they would see another round of ballots. If you want to see more campaign videos, visit the Yemi for Mayor page on YouTube.

Transparency and Accountability

There has been a growing epidemic of distrust in our government nationwide. It is a problem that I am sure we are not the only city to address. We wanted to bring accountability back to the forefront. Yemi never wanted the City Administration Building to feel like an untouchable ivory tower. He aims to be one of the most approachable and accessible mayors the city has ever seen. We started this trend during the campaign.

When I was telling you about our magnificent Communications Chair, Joe Hollmann, I told you about the campaign finance reports and how we brought those reports out of the shadows per se, and into the forefront of the race. We wanted people to have access and have the power to review those reports in an easy and consumable manner. We took the data and broke it down into bar graphs and charts that showed the numbers. We could tell our story through the finance reports and compare that story from the other camps. We could share the excitement of just how many unique donors we had in comparison and how much more widespread our donor base was. Our story was so impactful because our donor base was everyday citizens across all neighborhoods and parts of the city giving $20, $50, $100, or whatever they could afford to give. The citizens were fueling our campaign. They were telling the story of what they wanted their government to look like. It was not being driven by special interest. We used to say the only special interests we needed to answer to were the special interests of the citizens!

Transparency and accountability are so important to Yemi that he started his office as mayor by doing city wide listening tours while working through his First 100-day plan. He wanted to ensure his priorities as mayor are in direct alignment with the needs of the neighborhoods. He has even introduced a new practice in the mayor's office, delivering biweekly addresses to citizens through the city's social media platforms, where he shares updates on upcoming events, project progress, and more. It has made the city feel as though they are standing right there with him through his tenor.

This helped unite citizens behind a common cause. No matter what side of the aisle, no matter what race, color, creed, or so on, you knew that the best chance of your voice being heard in city government was with Yemi Mobolade at the helm.

Chapter Eight

Leadership Through Adversity

There Were No Rose Colored Glasses

B elieve me, this campaign was not all rainbows and butterflies. While we had a city rallying behind us in ways we could not have imagined, ruffling feathers with the powers that be often brings resistance. Not every single person in town was overjoyed at the attention we were getting from the public. We were seen as a threat to the established way of doing things. So, they pushed back—and they pushed back hard. When I spoke of the attack ads we received, they were interesting, to say the least. I found it ironic that they tried to label a pastor, small business owner, former small business development administrator for the city, and Chamber of Commerce employee as a socialist. It became a war of stereotypes. He is Black, an immigrant, and an independent—so clearly, he must be a socialist, right? Please. It was shameful. The attacks became increasingly vicious, portraying him as a far-left liberal socialist who would bring down the city. Because he said, 'I am neither Democrat nor Republican. I am for Colorado Springs. So, if you want, you can call me a Colorado Springs-ican or a Colorado Springs-ocrat.' I am sure that in our traditionally very conservative city, they thought that if they just started calling him the antithesis of all things conservative, everyone would just blindly follow their lead. We had far more faith in Colorado Springs voters. We believed they could think rationally for themselves, have a conversation with him and decide if they wanted to vote for him or not.

As a republican myself, if I took off my Campaign Manager hat and put on my Colorado Springs voter hat, I found it offensive. The assumption that I would fall for such blatant sensationalism, without considering my intelligence, was appalling. I have friends who are democrats, and I asked them, does painting him left wing in this manner make you want to vote for him? Even they admitted it just felt dirty and desperate.

But we rose above it. Endorsement after endorsement came from people who were the antithesis of socialists. What Yemi did was lead in a manner that was in consistent alignment with the mission. We stayed the course, managed the noise, and emphasized his policies on supporting small businesses in the community. We discussed our dedication to enhancing public safety and addressing issues related to the housing crisis.

When we discuss the struggles we endured, there was plenty to choose from. One story that I have debated back and forth with myself and my advisors on this book to even tell was one of those struggles. While I discuss it, what I will say is the focus of this will remain on the way Yemi led through it. During the campaign, I received a disturbing phone call about an incident involving one of our political signs. The incident was racially motivated and charged, inappropriate to say the very least. We worked quickly to address the issue. It was our hope and desire to protect others, to not give the incident any oxygen and just move about our day. What this deranged individual did could have sparked a racially charged incident, causing havoc in the city if the situation had not been managed correctly. While we quickly addressed the issue with the proper authorities, this person leaked a video to the media. Once the media got involved, we did everything we could to persuade them not to run the story, as it would only empower an unstable individual.

Because this might spark an incident in the city and, for the safety of the citizens, we wanted to stop that from happening. We had managed our own security internally, and we wanted to not give this any oxygen to protect the integrity of the race and not give power to someone who did not deserve to receive it. The media ran with the story, which is their right. While we disagreed, now what was more important was not letting this get sensationalized, keeping the city safe and detracting focus from the race.

Calling Yemi to inform him of what had happened was one of the hardest calls I ever had to make. Here was my friend and colleague—one of the best human beings I know—and I had to deliver this disheartening news. I explained the incident, that we had authorities involved and we needed him to know that we were working on a plan on how to manage the situation. My heart just sank. He sat there quietly for a moment, and he said, "We're not giving this oxygen. This is not the Colorado Springs I know, and we are not giving power to one individual who did something crazy." We had a debate that night that he needed to prepare for. I told him, 'I will manage the press. You focus on tonight, and we will move past this like we have moved past everything else.' Everyone will understand if you do not feel you want to discuss this. He said, "No. I need to be the one to address this. I will make the statement, and we will immediately shift focus back to the race. I need to lead my city through this." In true Yemi fashion, he rose to the occasion. He calmed fears, settled anxieties, gave it no fuel, and reminded everyone that there was a mayoral race to be run. We have a debate to focus on. That is what we should talk about and immediately went back to the issues. He managed the situation with grace and dignity. But continued to focus on issues such as mental health and addressing the needs of those in the community.

Another issue that occurred at the start of the campaign was the Club Q shooting. While Yemi was not in office during this tragedy, questions around it arose during forums and meet and greets. Yemi was gracious. He honored the lives lost in this horrific tragedy and focused on his goal of creating a city where all residents feel safe.

He honored the swift response times we saw from our Colorado Springs police and fire departments and the actions of the local heroes who stepped up to help amid the chaos. To this day, he continues to honor those affected and works tirelessly to create a safer city.

Fundraising

Fundraising was a nonstop, round-the-clock activity. Every single time somebody asked me what we needed, my answer was dollars and votes. We need donations and votes! Sometimes they just wanted to know what I needed for lunch, but that was always my answer! Because we were the disruptor in the race, we did not have big money being funneled into our campaign. We had several incredibly generous supporters, but we were not receiving the gigantic checks that some of our opponents were, and that was okay because it reinforced our story. When you are running a campaign on a much smaller budget, you get highly creative about how and what you spend it on. You become very streamlined and resourceful. We were up against entities willing to spend any amount of money to maintain the status quo. We were outspent by an exponential amount, but what I felt like we did very well was spend smart. Anthony deserves a lot of credit here. He figured out ways to get the biggest bang for our buck everywhere we could. I mentioned before, he would spend it, and I would raise it. He would come to me and say, 'I need this amount by the end of the week.' I would turn to our fundraising committee and to the community and get to work. We need to raise this much money to do this task. We reached out to every entity we knew and asked them who else might be able to help. This community is so generous! It always came through. People helped us find others who cared as much about this city as we did. There was no waste. Thomas, Anthony, and I were laughing while reminiscing during my preparation for this book. Thomas said, "Campaigning is so glamorous! Where else can you eat cold pizza, while sitting on a folding chair, at a folding table, while putting updated date stickers over old dates on cards!" We did not want to waste a thing! When we hit the runoff, we still had info cards left over with the original election date, so we had to change the date to the new runoff election date. What are you going to do? The sad part was that so many people wanted to help but were afraid to have their names on a finance report due to fear of backlash. But we managed just fine! Somehow, we spent less money and still won the day!

The age-old saying applies here: what you do in the face of adversity defines your character. What matters is what you make of the struggles and how you manage those crises. The blessing, I believe, was that we proved you can become highly resourceful and efficient. We wanted to honor every dollar that was donated so that we could go back to those donors and say here is how we spent those dollars and look at the difference your donation could make. The impact of each dollar grew significantly.

The last story I will tell here was a doozie. Remember when I told you how I told Yemi I want to finish this campaign with my dignity and integrity intact? He did too. From the beginning, we agreed we would rather lose with our values intact than win without them. Otherwise, what would it all be for? We were getting to the point of crunch time towards the end. We were spending money as fast as it came in—sometimes faster! The grind of raising money in those last few weeks was hard. We worked around the clock to ensure we had everything we needed and that we were streamlining spending as efficiently as we could. One afternoon, we were working out of the back meeting space at Wild Goose when my phone rang. I stepped outside to answer it. An individual in town we had been trying to get connected with, to no avail, reached out through a third party to donate a very sizable donation, approximately $200,000. I almost stopped breathing. He assured me that this individual was ready to make the donation.

I was already mentally spending that money, but his next sentence stopped my internal spending spree in its tracks. His request, per the donor, was that much of the donation had to be used as attack ads against the other candidate. He assured me it was the only way we could win. That we did not have a chance. His intention was more that he wanted to bring the other "powers that be" down. There were, of course, aspirations he had of his own and felt the other side was a roadblock. I paused, gathered my thoughts and I said, "No. We will not run any negative attack messaging. We have made a commitment to each other and the residents of this city that we will not go negative."

"We have repeatedly asked to meet with him to discuss Yemi's platform, but he has declined. Now, if he is on team Yemi, and genuinely believes that he is the best candidate for the city and is still wanting to make an outright donation, then that is one thing. But dictating that any portion of it at all is to be used for negative campaigning...well, then I politely decline the gift." He assured me I was making a huge mistake. That he knew we needed the money, but that he respected how I felt about it. I hung up the phone. I walked back into the meeting room with Yemi and said, "Well, if ever there was a day you wanted to fire me, today is probably the day to do it."

Yemi laughed, said, "Ok" and I told him what happened. He gave me a big hug and said, "You did exactly what I would have told you to do. We do not need it. We will figure it out. We always do." I never once questioned my decision and neither did Yemi. There will be times where temptation waves what you think is the answer to your immediate problem right in front of you. But be aware, taking the bait will make you question yourself, your integrity, and will only create much bigger problems later. Be strong and be a person of integrity. Always. I do not blame him. He thought it was the only way to win and that he could shepherd that process along. But a loss with your integrity is much sweeter than a win without it.

Chapter Nine

We Are Stronger Together
What Helped Seal the Deal

I have talked extensively about the unity we fostered during this campaign, and how we truly embodied the definition of a melting pot. We opened the doors to everyone, welcoming them in, creating a safe space, and giving them a voice. Mike Juran and Susan Pattee both commented on how much they loved the diversity of the people on the campaign, diversity of ages, gender, race, color, military, and political affiliation. Yemi can speak to both sides of the aisle and make space for each. There was no judgment, condemnation or exclusion. All are welcome. But what our campaign reflected was the city itself. Colorado Springs is a diverse city. The campaign simply reflected what was already happening here. Susan commented that Colorado Springs is a place where you can make your own story. We joke around here that nobody is from here, they just got here as fast as they could. But all the influx of people from various places has created a city of every kind of background. The beauty of a melting pot.

The Campaign Culture

One of the greatest strengths I think we had was the campaign culture itself. Our culture was one of inclusion, but the camaraderie we shared was unmatched. We were a "Campaign of Yes." Yes, you are home here. Yes, we will find a place for you. Yes, we will welcome your thoughts and concerns. Yes, yes, yes. Every person on this campaign knew that everything they did mattered. We had little money, so we stickered cards. We did not have a huge marketing budget, so we door knocked. We were as grassroots as it comes but what that does is facilitate bonding and building a culture. Our culture was based on the belief that if we stuck together and worked hard, we could cross the finish line strong. The story we wanted to tell was that hard work, dedication, and teamwork matter. Thomas Thompson told me, "I knew we would outwork everyone." We were not afraid to roll up our sleeves and get the job done.

Yemi was not a lazy candidate. He put the same amount of work in for 1 or 2 people as he did for a city of 500,000+ residents. It did not matter how big or small the task, we put 100% in because Yemi put 100% in. Yemail "Yemi" Sanchez, (remember I told you we had two Yemi's - but we called her Sanchez!) told me she vividly remembers Anthony's speeches to the team towards the end of the campaign. He gave the dad speeches, she said! Haha! "We have a finite date when everything we do pays off, or it doesn't. Do you want to be sitting there on election night wishing you had pushed a little harder? Wishing you had done more. 'Should I have called one more person? Should I have knocked on one more door?' You do not want to be thinking that on election night!" She laughed because she was tired, but also knew he was right. I mean it every single time I say that my team was the hardest working team in politics. But it created so much comradery. Every time we thought we hit our limit, together we found another level to push through. We got smarter and scrappier. It was easier to push ourselves because Yemi was right there with us every step of the way.

People would tell us they hated politics, but that this was different. They got involved deeply because this was about shaping the future of our city. Even when they were nervous about door knocking, they would go out nevertheless with a buddy and hit every door. For one, doing it together created its own bonding experience, but they knew everyone needed to hear how Yemi was different. That the city could be different. They knew it mattered. In fact, we had an older gentleman call us and he told us that a lovely young lady knocked on his door to tell him about Yemi. She was so sweet and kind, and obviously extremely nervous, but it was so inspiring to him. He told us if this young lady could muster up the courage and be so brave to knock on a stranger's door, that whatever she had to say must be important. Whoever this guy was must be different. "It was because of her I voted for Yemi." Here I go welling up again!

Quickly, I must tell you. Door knocking with Yemi was always fun. We went out together. People would answer the door and instantly the shocked face would appear. "Hey, you're the guy from TV. You are running for mayor, right? I have never had a mayor knock on my door! Have I got some questions for you!" And he would take all the time to answer their questions and address their concerns. We had the best conversations out knocking. People often said, 'I am going to tell my friends. Thank you for taking the time to talk with me.' But he relished the opportunity to visit with them. He would even run back by and bring yard signs when they requested one. He would even put them up for them.

Campaign of Integrity

What resonated with people was our steadfast commitment to running a campaign of integrity. There were no "campaign promises," no special interest groups, no back door deals. Everything we said and did, we said and did in front of the community. We stressed the importance of transparency and them understanding every aspect of our work. I think we can all agree that the citizens have lost faith in their government. A huge part of Yemi's goal is to help restore that trust. It is why he puts so much time and energy into transparency and reporting out to the city. During the campaign, we laid the groundwork for that rebuilding of trust. We wanted to ensure they knew Yemi was approachable and accessible, that we understood their pain points, and that they were being heard. What still stands out to me is how Yemi would take notes during every conversation he had. He would pull out his phone and make notes so that he would forget nothing. In fact, I laugh because I remember this one time we were meeting with a constituent, and he pulled his phone out like he always did and was taking notes. I looked up, and the person had a funny look on their face, and I realized what they were thinking. "He likes to take notes so that he forgets nothing. He wants to make sure that he gets back to you on everything you are asking about. He's not texting." And we all had a good laugh! From that day on, he would always say when he was with someone and he pulled his phone out, "I like to take notes. I'm not texting." Haha! It was so funny! People would laugh all the time. But every time, he would come to me within a few days and say, "We need to get this info back to so and so. I don't want them thinking I forgot." When one of us would reach back out to them to get them whatever they asked for, they were always shocked. They could not believe we followed through on their request. "I never thought I would hear from him again. He'll be getting my vote." That personalized attention he has carried into the mayor's office.

The Values Based Campaign

In the beginning of the book, I discussed Courage, Empathy and Humility. I spoke here on integrity. But I think another core value we had was trust. The trust that Yemi, Anthony and I had to have in each other was immense. We knew that if we had each other's backs, no matter what, nothing could break the three of us. We knew we would be attacked. People would try to break us in order to break the campaign and we would not let that happen. We trusted each other's intentions and remembered that our shared goal was always the same. We had to exemplify all these values to instill them in our team. We were also asking a lot from people, and we needed them to trust us and our leadership so that they, too, could push through and exhibit those same values. Everyone on the team understood that at the end of the day, they reflected Yemi in the community. We all wanted to honor that and represent him in a way that showed his values and pride. I would work with those two men anytime and would not hesitate to stand by them.

A True Independent

I feel as if our campaign demonstrated the true nature of an independent, nonpartisan campaign. I am here to tell you folks; it CAN be done. We believed in telling the story of better governance, and this campaign proved it is possible. There does not have to be conflict or a contradiction of values—just open, respectful dialogue between different points of view. There can be a world where we see all sides of the political spectrum. As a republican I can stand here and say, yes, I have strong views on some issues that for me are values based and issues of my moral code. There are issues I will always vote for or against because that is my right as an American citizen. But that does not mean I cannot have open, respectful dialogue with people who hold opposing views. Conversation is how we all learn and grow. But what we have lost sight of is that most people agree on most issues. Yes, there are going to be those issues that we will never agree completely on and is that not great that in a free America we have the right to disagree...respectfully? What has happened is we have let "big government" take the few issues that are so divisive and use those to drive wedges and create havoc. They have highlighted those few issues to keep us fighting amongst ourselves. Do not get me wrong, I believe in standing up and fighting for what is right and fighting for an issue. But we have lost the ability to be passionate while still being respectful and showing dignity to the other person. Fighting for an issue is quite different from attacking another person. They are not the same. Be passionate, be a patriot, stand up for your beliefs. Absolutely! Do not get soft and complacent. But for the love of Pete, do it with dignity and respect. My momma always said the saying, you can catch more flies with honey than vinegar. Vinegar has infiltrated our country, and we must stop it. At the end of the day, things have gotten big, out of control and there is only so much we can do. But you always have control over yourself, the way you respond and the way you react. You have control over your own behavior. I know at the day of my judgment the only actions I must answer for are mine, so I better do the best I can with what I have control over today.

Our Advisory Board

There are no words to express my gratitude to our advisory board. We had leaders of industry, entrepreneurs, and people with a passion for a brighter city. Everyday citizens who believed in a better way to govern. The board had a bird's-eye view of watching Yemi grow even more as a leader. And they helped foster that growth. Yemi was a strong candidate no doubt, but what he understands better than anyone is you are stronger with a formidable team around you. He brought the right people together who could push him and challenge him in ways he may not even thought possible. He knew these people would make him better, make us better, and help us cross the finish line. These people became our sounding board, our place to rest and, honestly, my sense of strength and perseverance. The 36 hours surrounding the sign incident were the hardest hours of the entire campaign for me. Watching my friend being attacked, dealing with the fallout, becoming the human shield for Yemi, and dealing with all the moving pieces around that was painful. I was on high alert, no time for emotions, no time for the tears we all wanted to shed. We just had to focus on getting through it. I mentioned that night was a major debate. We had to push through all that while getting through the debate. At the back of the stage, I was reeling with fielding phone calls and dealing with the issue at hand. At the end of the debate, when everything was done and the dust was settling, I turned around, made eye contact with Thomas, and burst into tears. The emotional release was long overdue. He grabbed my shoulders, looked me in the eye and said, "I'm going to stand here with you until you get it all out. Sometimes we forget how much this stuff affects you, too." I will forever call Thomas my friend.

Him and Mike, those poor guys got my waterworks more than most! After another grueling day, I walked into Mike's office and burst into tears again! Haha! He was so sweet. He said, "I have food, you need to eat" and gave me a big hug! My cup runneth over with the love and support I received from that entire group of friends, mentors, and advisors. Every one of them had moments with Yemi, Anthony and I where they picked us up, dusted us off and said, "We have you."

It is hard to do justice in explaining the value the board provided. They gave Yemi, Anthony and I a safe space to process our thoughts. Sometimes, they simply gave us the space we needed. A place where we could share our wins and losses and just decompress. They provided clear strategic vision and could speak wisdom into every conversation. They helped with strategic connections, they supported us financially and helped justify decisions. We never felt alone with them at our backs. When we felt attacked, they were there. When we needed to talk through something, they were there. When I had those moments of snotty girl sobbing, they were there. Every one of them I will forever call, friend.

Between the board and the volunteer team, we truly had the Dream Team.

Chapter Ten

The Win

Part of Something Bigger

At 44, Yemi Mobolade became the 42nd Mayor of Colorado Springs. I enjoy recounting the events of election night, both for the general and the runoff. The night of the general, there were still twelve candidates in the running, but we knew there were two others to beat. We anticipated a long night and came prepared. In Colorado Springs, a single candidate must win 50% +1 of the votes to win and not go to a runoff. We knew in a field of twelve that 50% +1 would be hard to get. So, we hunkered down, ready for the long night ahead. We stood in a room with what I believe was around eight hundred or more people at the general election night watch party. We honored door knockers that had hit 1,000+ doors a piece. We even had a couple of ladies in their seventies who were knocking on just as many doors! We prepared a video, fully expecting the night to be long. We had the screens up and ready. We told folks to be prepared. This may take a while. As we prepared for the first round of results to come in, we all stared at the screen with hopeful anticipation. What we did not expect was to be leading the pack by double digits right out of the gate. That night we advanced to the runoff with a 29.81% lead over our next closest competitor at 19.22%. We were floored! The overwhelming excitement in the room felt like it could have blown the roof off the building! We all sat back and realized that this was real. That this was happening. Yemi stood up, gave an awe-inspiring speech, and reminded us that the work was not done. That we now had 6 more weeks to drive even harder. This next leg of the race would be the fight of our lives, and we had to see it through to the very end, strong and determined.

Sanchez told me that this was the moment it all hit her, and everything became real. She said, "We're going to win this. We have to get ready." The city had spoken, and we advanced to the runoff by a landslide. That night, we realized we had shifted the power dynamic and were changing the political landscape. When Joe Hollmann and I chatted about the book, I asked him why he got involved. He said, "It was time to disrupt the power dynamics in the city." This city had been so heavily influenced by special interest groups, and the people of Colorado Springs deserved better. "We needed to level the playing field," he said. We wanted to show that an underdog could win, and we wanted to give power back to those who did not have it. We wanted to show that character matters in our elected officials. The people wanted it too, and they had spoken.

The period between the general election and the runoff was twice as intense as the general election itself. On top of interviews, campaigning, door knocking, and a myriad of other activities, we would have anywhere from 3 to 5 meets and greets a day. We all had that finite day in the back of our minds, and we were going to give it everything we had all the way across the finish line. The numbers of people wanting Yemi's attention doubled or even tripled. We were even more determined to ensure that every ear heard his name and every citizen who wanted to learn more had that opportunity. Also, when you head to a runoff, all the endorsements reset. Everyone was now looking at the two remaining candidates in the race to see who they were going to support. In Colorado Springs, there was a trend where the candidate endorsed by the big institutions was expected to win by default. Without their endorsement, you were not seen as a contender. We did not have any of the big institutional endorsements. And we did not mind. Our endorsements came from individuals—people out in the community doing the real work. They were the ones down in the trenches. Every time an "institution" gave their endorsement to our competitor, it fueled our story. We could say, "We are not a part of the machine, the special interests' groups or the status quo." It helped us tell our story even stronger that Yemi was a candidate of the people. You can have power and influence and not be a part of the special interests.

Election Night

May 16, 2023, was the night that all our lives were changed. The night that changed the future of Colorado Springs. I will never forget that night as long as I live. There were about 1,000 people at the watch party. Every background, race, political affiliation, and age group was represented. The diversity of the crowd was overwhelming. People were smiling, laughing, hugging. The excitement was more than you could absorb. Once again, we were prepared for a long night. As I got up to make my speech about halfway through my remarks, I heard this giant yell from the back of the room! The early numbers were starting to drop! You can imagine what was going through my head while I was trying to finish my remarks! I finished my speech, handed the mic back to our emcee for the next portion of the program and hurried off the stage. Anthony came running up to me and said you will not believe the numbers! We were already over 50%! In my shock I said, "Are we calling it?!!" And Anthony screamed, "Yes, yes!" We both went running to the staging room where we had Yemi and his family waiting. I ran to Yemi and grabbed him and said, "We did it, friend! We did it!!!" Yemi sat back, completely speechless. We all cried and rejoiced! It was real! Yemi Mobolade was the 42nd Mayor of Colorado Springs. All the sleepless nights, cold pizza and door knocking in the freezing cold paid off!!! We could not believe it happened. Someone turned to Abbey and said, "Would you like to be the first to call him by his new name?" Abbey turned to

Yemi, put her hands on his face and said, "Mr. Mayor. You did it." Everyone burst into tears. It was the emotional release of realizing that everything we had worked so hard for had come to fruition. Yemi won 57.5% over the opponents 42.5%.

When Yemi walked out on that stage as our emcee, Jay Dial announced, "Colorado Springs! Let me introduce you to your 42nd Mayor, Yemi Mobolade!" that room erupted! The energy, tears, laughter, and companionship were beyond words. I still get choked up when I remember that night. People were speechless. They had done it. Colorado Springs had spoken. They wanted change, and they got it. Yemi stood there for the longest time, just soaking up the moment. His heart was bursting with joy, excitement, and gratitude. It was a magical scene to watch. I cannot tell you how many hugs and congratulations we received that night. The thank you's and the pride people expressed will forever ring in my ears. It was indeed...a new day in Colorado Springs.

As Yemi gave his speech, he reiterated the work that he would do. The city we could all imagine becoming was in our grasp. That the only special interest was the people's interest. That now was the time the real work began. He thanked everyone for showing up, for giving so much of themselves and for showing the power of what people getting involved can produce. It was a night I will never forget.

No Time for Rest

Yemi immediately went to work. It would be approximately 3 weeks until his official swearing in, but he got to work. We had the framework for his first one hundred days. He immediately started meeting with his department heads and city staff. He started acting towards setting in motion the plans he had discussed on the campaign trail. There was no rest or downtime. He was on the job and ready to make an impact. The city rallied around him. The media swarmed at him. We had interview requests from across the nation...even the globe! Dignitaries from across the country reached out to congratulate him, and they were in awe of what we accomplished. There was not time to soak in what we had done. I do not think that we even realized what we had done until months later. Even today I still cannot soak it all in sometimes. But we did do it. We showed it is possible to make a difference in your community. You do not have to sit back and watch your communities cater to specific groups. It was a Cinderella story of sorts.

The Legacy

When Sanchez and I were visiting about this project, she gave me the most beautiful perspective of our journey. We were discussing why she got involved in the first place. She told me she hated politics before this. But something about Yemi was different. She said she realized she was at a point in her life where she had to help create the city she wanted to live in, and Yemi was the catalyst for that change. She is a first generation American and was always a responsible and educated voter. She said, "I'm the next generation. Whoever wins this race will shape the future for the city and I will be the next generation of citizens to help continue whatever we do here. But if I get involved, I can help shape it too. Once the city is handed to my generation, it will be our turn to be good stewards of what we were handed. Even if we are not the decision makers, we need to be in those spaces where those decision makers are. We will then pass the baton to the generation after us (a little nod to Olympic City there!)." Yemi fully understands the importance of the role he plays in inspiring the next generation. He will only be in office for 4-8 years and he wants to ensure that the future leaders of the city will be ready to stand up and create the city they want, a city for the many, not the few. Whether through leading in adversity or rising above division to unite, Yemi understands that every move we make now affects future generations. He has carried all our values from the campaign trail into the mayor's office: Courage, Empathy, Humility, Trust, Transparency and Unity.

The Call to Action

I want to first stress to you that you do not have to have our Yemi to do this in your city. You have the power to be the change. WHAT we accomplished here was so much bigger than WHO accomplished it. While Yemi is an extraordinary candidate, one of my dearest friends, a man of faith, unity, and force for good, the people of the city are the real heroes. The people who spoke out and said we want different, better, for our city. The people who sacrificed so much to be a part of this journey because they were inspired and wanted more for their home. They are the real heroes. The citizens of Colorado Springs came together and declared they would no longer stand for division and special interests. We want a city that hears the cries of its people and responds accordingly.

I was told by Joe that he had always felt like this city had a "cool kids' table" and that table was not welcoming. That it was reserved for the few and the elite. I told him what I felt like we did was open the whole cafeteria and made all the people "cool kids." We highlighted the people who were doing the work of making this city the best it could be. We invited them all to the decision-making table. For the people who said, we want a city for the people and by the people, I commend you. If you cannot find your "Yemi" in your town, be the "Yemi." Be the person who leads and unites. Who ignites a fire inside people to get involved and speak up. And if you take nothing else from the book, take this; Get Involved. Become an educated voter and, most importantly...show up! Show up on election day and cast your ballot for what you believe in. VOTE! It is one of the greatest rights we have as American citizens. Do not let it go to waste.

Also by the Author

Thriving in Salon Ownership:
What They Don't Teach You
About Owning A Salon

Keeping Promises
(co-authored with her mother and sister)

Connect with Niki

Looking for a guest speaker or an author visit? Please get in touch for availability and details.

WEBSITE AND SOCIAL MEDIA

https://nikicicak.com/

https://www.linkedin.com/in/niki-cicak/

https://www.instagram.com/nikicicak

https://x.com/nikicicak